META-GAZING

META-GAZING

(A mind that sees beyond phenomenal realities)

Stephen Touthang

First Published, 2021

Published by

Kalpaz Publications
C-30, Satyawati Nagar,
Delhi – 110052
Ph.: 011-47034999, 9811692060
www.kalpazpublications.com
E-mail: kalpaz@hotmail.com

Printed at: Gyan Press, Delhi.

Cataloging in Publication Data—DK

Courtesy: D.K. Agencies (P) Ltd. <docinfo@dkagencies.com>

Touthang, Stephen, author.

Meta-gazing : a mind that sees beyond phenomenal realities / Stephen Touthang.

pages cm

ISBN 9789353246365 (HB)

1. Life. 2. Motivation (Psychology) 3. Self-culture. I. Title.

LCC BD431.T68 2021 | DDC 128 23

Life is short.

I am only a passer-by in this world. Whatever good I want to do, I must do it now and whatever good I want to say, I must say it now and whatever good I want to give, I must give it now for I am not going to pass this way again. All that I do is valedictory because I will not get the same opportunity again.

Author

Contents

Foreword

Many of us look at persons and judge them according to our own perceptions, by how we see them behave or act externally. This also applies to different situations and events we encounter in our life. We, not only see persons specifically but we also see ourselves superficially. We fail to gaze or look beyond what appears. *Meta-Gazing* is a very interesting book through which the author underscores the need *"to gaze beyond because there is always the other side or deeper side of every person."* The author, writing this book in an anecdotal style, tries to inspire the reader to a more reflective life, to recognize the element of what lies beyond in every person, to break the barrier of normal or common type in order to see deeper side of life, to be able to see who he/she really is beyond his/her appearance. When you take interest in persons, that is looking at them as subjects not as objects, we can discover the reality of the person, a wealth of beautiful things in the person, which will lead us to understand life in a more objective manner and we become more humane and human towards other people, to be more compassionate and empathetic towards fellow human beings and to nature, that is all life is about.

Anecdote has been a source of inspiration to the millions of people at all times. The book *Meta-Gazing*, written in an anecdotal style is strongly motivational in nature and will definitely inspire many youth and educationists and help to appreciate other persons, to be more objective in their evaluation of situations and events.

There are many young people weight down by depression due to unprecedented problems in the family, troubles in the society and unsuccessful life story. However, while some have failed in the situation itself, the others celebrated their triumph over them by looking beyond the deeper side of the situations. We need to gaze beyond what we see and feel because every person and situation is unique and different in its own way. Therefore, we need to look beyond the world of mere appearances. And when we are ready to gaze beyond, we will come to know the deeper side of human beings and their situations.

Life becomes richer and meaningful when we enter deeper into our own inner self to see the reality that we are in. We remain on superficial level and our judgment becomes superficial and shallow because "we look at the appearance but God looks at the heart" says the Bible.

Reading this book will certainly enhance the reader's life and outlook and positively enrich his/her life and contribute towards making the life of others richer and meaningful.

Most Rev. Dominic Lumon D.D
Archbishop of Imphal
Manipur, India

Introduction

It is de rigueur for every human being to interact with other human beings, situations and events. One can't escape from this phenomenon. Sociality and gregariousness are part of human nature itself. The people, situations and events that one comes across in the labyrinth of one's daily life may not be pleasant always because every person, every event or situation that one encounters is unique and different. This is because every human being is unique and therefore his interaction with other people, situation and event will also be different. As a consequence, one cannot expect that every interaction will be always smooth, fluid, congenial and pleasant. Due to this, one can be driven into the vortex of relational chaos and at times he or she can be completely distraught and bogged down to a frazzle. There are so many people who are buried alive in the avalanche of depression. Situations and events are nature's providence through which human beings are tested, purified and elevated. Some have failed and died in the situation itself while others celebrate their triumph over them. Therefore, we will be able to deal with different persons and situations successfully if we are ready to look beyond the superficial. We need to gaze beyond because there is always *the other side or deeper side* of every person, event and situation. This is called META-GAZING (gazing beyond). This is a deeper analysis and understanding of a person, situation or event. So, whenever you face a person or an event, always look beyond what you see. This will help you to understand deeper the person and the situation. Never judge a person or situation at the *prima facie* appearance but view a little deeper than what you see. How can you get the target when your eyes are so fixed on the arrow and not on the Bull's eye? Some people are so fixed on the arrow that they forget or miss the target. They are not able to gaze beyond.

We need to gaze beyond what we see and feel. We need to look beyond the world of mere appearances. Today, the world is pervaded with hate, misunderstanding, violence, misery, chaos, and selfishness because we are not able to analyze and understand the deeper side of events and people. We are not even ready or willing to gaze beyond. When we are ready to gaze beyond, we will come to know the deeper side of every human being and their situation. In the Bible, there is a story of the Good Samaritan who looks beyond. The story runs thus:

> *Once a Jewish man was going down from Jericho to Jerusalem, he was attacked by brigands on the way and he laid half-dead in the corner of the road. Now, a priest was passing by. He saw the man bleeding but avoided and walked away. Next came the Levite, he also did as the first. Finally, a Samaritan came, saw the man bleeding and lying half-dead. He took him, washed the wounds and applied balm over it and gave him the best care possible.*

The first two escaped from the person and the situation without responding. But the Good Samaritan faced the person and the situation and tried his best to save the wounded person. He could also avoid easily and escape but he didn't! He went beyond. How did he go beyond? By going beyond the boundaries of his tribe, community, culture, language, religion, and region. This is a deeper understanding of the person and situation that he encountered. The Jews considered the Samaritans as outcasts. The Jews and Samaritans were congenital enemies and they had nothing in common. The Good Samaritan as soon as he saw the wounded man, he didn't first enquire who the wounded man was? Was he a Jew or Samaritan? He didn't bother about the wounded man's socio-cultural affiliations. All his concern was to save the person's life. The most important thing to do at that moment was to save the person without reference to culture, tribe, community, language or region. The Good Samaritan is a paragon of one who looks beyond. It was the Good Samaritan's attitude of *gazing beyond* that changed the whole situation. In this book you will come across anecdotal reflections which will help you to see a deeper level of encountering people, situations and events of life.

1

Adversity

"Adversity causes some men to break; others to break records."
– Henry Arthur Ward

Adversity brings out the best in a person. The function of adversity in human life is to unfold the true and authentic nature of a person. Adversity tests a person's probity and inner strength. It is an ineluctable reality that has to be encountered by every being that is in being. A few men have met this monster boldly and have celebrated their victory over it. Contrariwise, a myriad of people, who try to eschew have only made abortive attempts to overcome it. The famous Romantic poets in English literature, who were also known as 'escapists' were not able to face the adversities of life and so they made umpteen essays to escape. They use 'imagination' as an instrument to transport themselves from the world of realities to the world of nature. This is the reason why they were called "Romanticists". Wordsworth escaped and resided in the lap of nature, S. T. Coleridge ran pell-mell from the monster and escaped to the Middle Ages and resided amidst the ruins of the castles and fortresses and had a tryst with the medieval romances and adventures. While John Keats, the youngest of the Romantic poets, flew away 'on the wings of poesy' and lived in the world of the Nightingale. Nevertheless, such escapism proved only temporary and soon they were transported back to the stark realities of life.

Escaping from adversity proves only ephemeral and transitory. The only and real way to escape from adversity is by facing it. It is said that the Juniper plant smells sweetest when flung into flames. Likewise, adversity should bring out the best essence in us. Adversity should not be deemed as 'coarse monster' but as a 'benevolent rogue' for without it, nobody can bring out the best in themselves. Like the Juniper plant, when adversity strikes us, we should emit fragrance of love, peace, patience, kindness, joy, and determination. Remember the words of C.C. Colton, *"Adversity misunderstood becomes a double curse"*.

2

Ahimsa

> *"Ahimsa is not mere negative non-injury. It is positive, cosmic love. It is the development of mental attitude in which hatred is replaced by love. Ahimsa is true sacrifice. Ahimsa is forgiveness. Ahimsa is Sakti (power). Ahimsa is true strength."* – **Sivananda**

Ahimsa is an evergreen word that needs to be internalized and actualized in our day to day living. *"Mentally don't injure others"* is the basic creed of Ahimsa. The *Rishis* of the old had already commended this perennial value of life to be lived at the psychological mind-space. Living Ahimsa at the psychological mind-space means that we should never exude "psychological invective – mentally, we should never curse anyone, never wish harm to anybody."

Ahimsa does not mean "non-killing" or "non-injury" at the physical level. Sometimes, if need be, physical cruelty and injury must be done, even though we may be packed with inner qualities of love and kindness. Therefore, Ahimsa is to be understood as a mental attitude to our relationship with others in life. Shakespeare has beautifully expressed this idea in his play *"Hamlet"*, *"I am cruel only to be kind."* For example, a surgeon may appear cruel and bloody while performing surgery but his heart targets "well-being."

This message of Ahimsa is not to be preached but to be lived. It is a practical message and not an abstract concept.

Ahimsa must be taken as a personal belonging and should become part and parcel of one's life. Remember, while serving the world in the spirit of Ahimsa, we may have to inflict minor pains but its aim should be to bless them. Let us follow the footprints of Gandhi. Like him, we must try our best to inflict pain to the negative forces operating within a person but not injure him. Ahimsa is therefore a battle against evil. We must aim at rooting out these evils so that we can bless a person with our love. Therefore, Ahimsa is all about purifying others by fighting and removing the evil that is within a person without harming him or her. It is all about eradicating the evil within a person and creating a conducive environment for the person to grow morally and spiritually. Practicing Ahimsa can usher us into a new world of peace and prosperity.

3

Albert Schweitzer

One of the best biographies I have ever read is that of Albert Schweitzer. Albert Schweitzer was a multi-dimensional man of genius, who threw away his brilliant career to become one of the first doctors in the French Equatorial Africa. His cardinal belief was *"Reverence for life."* Dr. Howard A. Rusk wrote about him in the *New York Times* thus, *"Few men in history have equaled his achievements. He was supreme as a theologian, musician, scholar, philosopher, and a missionary bringing healing and understanding to French Equatorial Africa"*. In 1947, *Life* magazine described him as the greatest man in the world. As a brilliant scientist, Albert Einstein wrote to him a year later, *"You are one of the few who combine extraordinary energy and many-sidedness with the desire to serve man and to lighten his lot."* The African natives for whom he sacrificed his life were very fond of him and love him so much so that they told him, *"When you die, we will have a tom-tom of a week to mourn you."* He jokingly replied, *"Fortunately, I won't hear it."* In 1952, Albert Schweitzer's love for peace reached the acme when he was awarded the Nobel Prize for Peace. While he was a college student, his fellow students used to ask him, "How did you manage to do so much?" Usually, he only laughed. But if they pressed him, he showed them a poem cut out of a French calendar, which he had framed and hung up above his work table:

Higher, ever higher,
Let thy dreams and wishes rise,
Let them mount like flame of fire,
Upwards to the skies.

Higher, ever higher,
And when the heaven is overcast,
May thy star of faith aspire
Till all is bright at last.

For more than sixty years this extract from a calendar was Schweitzer's inspiration. It is still to be found, faded, above his writing-desk in Gunsbach (a village in France).

Some of his important quotes:

- "I did not look forward to going to school, when on a fine October day my father for the first time put a slate under my arm and led me to the school mistress. I cried the whole way there, for I suspected that an end had now come to my dreams and my glorious freedom."
- "Man can no longer live for himself alone. We must realise that all life is valuable and that we are united to all life."
- "Just as while light consists of coloured rays, so Reverence for Life contains all the components of ethics: love, kindness, sympathy, empathy, peacefulness, and power to forgive."
- "Example is not the main thing in influencing others. It is the only thing."
- "A great secret of success is to go through life as a man who never gets used up."
- "A man does not have to be an angel in order to be a saint."
- "Therefore, search and see if there is not some place where you may invest your humanity."

- "You don't live in a world all alone. Your brothers are here too."
- "You must give sometime to your fellow men. Even if it's a little thing, do something for others – something for which you get no pay but the privilege of doing it."

4

A Mission to Save And Not to Destroy

"The most important thing for us is to save lives."
– Rick Perry, 47th Governor of Texas

Once, a hardcore militant of a certain unlawful organisation operating in Northeastern part of India had visited a priest in his parish. The priest was familiar with the militant as he had been visited by the militant quite a number of times. They had a very candid confabulation one day. Then, the militant narrated the long chain of dangerous adventures he had gone through to the priest. Above all these, he told the priest that in his organisation, one gains rank by the number of soldiers and people he kills. The priest looking at him carefully saw a special mark attached to his shirt inquired what it was! The militant answered that it was his designation. The priest said, "What is your designation?" "Commanding Officer" said his friend. The priest asked, "How did you manage to gain such a high echelon in your organisation?" "By killing" replied his friend. "O, God!" sighed the priest. Seeing his friendliness, the priest said to him, "I count the rank of a person by number of lives he has saved."

True greatness lies in saving others and not in killing. The greatest mission on earth is to save lives. The mission of every great person in history has been the redemption of mankind.

Let's us not shirk our fraternal responsibility like Cain who murdered his own brother Abel. When God asked him where his brother was? Cain answered, "Am I my brother's keeper?" (Genesis 4:9). God demanded accountability and Cain could not escape from his responsibility of protecting his brother. Each of us are our brother's keeper and we are accountable and responsible in protecting the lives of every human being.

5

A Nice Word Can Change a Person

Words can heal you. Words can kill you. Words can motivate you. Words can discourage you. Words can build you. Words can break you. Words can make you memorable. Words can vanish you forever. Because words travel to heart before reaching ears."

– Nashra Nazim

A young lad name Ricky used to weep soppily whenever he looked at his face in the mirror. One day the mother saw this and asked him, "Son, why do you weep every time you are in front of the mirror?" "Mom, I feel so ugly and nobody likes me". This lad had a fixed opinion about his image, that he is one farthest from handsome. But to his surprise one day a nice-looking girl told him, "Ricky, you are so nice and handsome!" After he heard these words from the girl, he ran back home and went straight to the mirror and began to cry very loud. Hearing such a loud crying, his mother rushed in and asked him, "Son! Why are you crying? What has happened to you?" "Mom, today I feel so happy because I have come to know that I am very handsome. This makes me cry very loudly", replied the boy.

- *Just a few nice words are sufficient to light up the whole life of a person.*

6

Are You Really Happy?

"The happiness of your life depends upon the quality of your thoughts: therefore, guard accordingly and take care that you entertain no notions unsuitable to virtue and reasonable nature."

– Marcus Aurelius

To be happy I need to know what actually happiness is! According to Wikipedia, *"Happiness is a state of mind or feeling characterised by contentment, love, satisfaction, pleasure or joy."* According to Abraham Lincoln, *"People are as happy as they make up their minds to be."*

Analysis of these two definitions:

(a) *"state of mind":* This means happiness is an interior phenomenon that happens in the mind and not outside of it. It is an inside job. Happiness is the condition of the mind.

(b) *"make up their minds...":* Here, happiness means deciding to be happy. If I want to be happy, it depends on me. It is about altering my mind to a better state. It means choosing things (better thoughts) judiciously that will take me to a better state of mind (happiness). Therefore, happiness means decision. It is choosing one's thoughts which are positive that will make me truly happy. Wrong choice will lead me to unhappiness and sometimes destruction too.

(c) *"feeling characterised by contentment, love..."*: According Wikipedia, happiness includes positive feelings. Feelings also begin from within. Feelings are the result of one's thoughts. Positive thoughts create positive feelings and negative thoughts give birth to negative feelings. Feelings are ignited by thoughts. Thoughts are formed by our experiences which we get through sensation or perception. It is the mind that receives the outside information, processes it and finally, it is manifested into feelings. It means the external data are translated into thoughts and thoughts are expressed into feelings. Therefore, it is the duty of the mind to process the data positively that will lead to happiness. Happiness is caused by positive feelings of love, contentment, satisfaction, joy, and peace.

Through analysis we have found that Happiness is an inside reality. If it is a positive interior environment, it depends on each one of us either to be happy or not to be happy. Now, if Happiness is within me, then, how can I find or discover that happiness? In order to find happiness, I need to introspect or retire into myself and examine what is going on within my interior world. There, you have to find out what kind of thoughts you often entertain - positive or negative. And if you are often given to negative thoughts, you need to transform them into positive ones. There are two types of feelings – positive and negative. The negative feelings are to be controlled and tamed; while, the positive feelings are to be galvanised into action. These positive feelings are like feelings of love, compassion, forgiveness, peace, joy and so on. If these feelings are not shown in action they are as good as death. But when you show them to someone who needs your love, care, help, sympathy, compassion, and forgiveness, you will automatically experience happiness. Happiness will come to you and you need not look for happiness. Happiness happens i.e., when you love, forgive, help, and share automatically happiness comes to you.

You cannot go on a hunting expedition in search of happiness. You cannot seek happiness; you have to make it happen because it is within you.

In today's world of instant solution, the problem lies when there is a plethora of self-help books or better yourself books and self-styled gurus dishing out their intellectual acumen and expertise on how to be happy and as a result, people don't feel the need for inner-engineering (finding happiness inside). It is a waste of time for them to take the inside journey. They look for short-cut methods for happiness which doesn't work for long. No one has time to examine oneself. The irony is that people look for happiness equation given by somebody else in the books and forget that they themselves are the happiness they are seeking for. They are the people who come from the land of oblivion.

Let us see how different people look at happiness!

The British Government had already started teaching Happiness classes in schools. The government has been advised to use advertising and marketing techniques to sell happier behaviour. The Wellington College already introduced lessons in well-being and positive psychology a few years ago and is extending classes to parents also. All these courses on happiness are designed to cheer up people and increase national optimism. Happiness classes will train children to be happy and will also encourage them to become more self-oriented. One of Britain's leading public schools has decided to conduct classes on cheerfulness and contentment as motivational gurus believe the time has come to teach happiness.

However, the surprising thing is that even after popping be-happy pills, the destination still remains hazy. According to a model-turn-agony aunt, Saira Mohan, this happens because we don't know what makes us happy anymore. She says, *"In a world driven by money, ambition and sex, happiness is fleeting and rare. Even when we find happiness, there is imbalance. Rarely is material happiness followed by emotional and spiritual happiness. What we essentially need to do is manage our happiness quotient.*" Here, we see that material happiness seldom effectuates emotional and spiritual happiness. We know that as Saira Mohan says happiness that comes from material things is fleeting or temporary and so it cannot fulfill or satisfy us permanently. If material things like money and wealth can give us real happiness why should the richest people in the world today are yet to acknowledge that real and authentic happiness comes from wealth and money? This is true of Bill Gates, a computer nerd, Microsoft chairman and co-founder.

According to *Forbes'* 2016 list of the world's billionaires, Mr. Gates is the richest person in the United States for the 17th time in a row with an estimated worth of 45 billion dollars. His possession includes a 40,000 sq.ft lake-side home in Washington State, a private library, 18-hole miniature golf course, a cinema and 24 bathrooms. His collection of art and books includes the Codex Leicester, the writings of Leonardo da Vinci, bought for

30.8 million dollars. Today, his wealth may afford him one of the most valuable houses on the globe, own some of the rarest books and audiences with the most powerful people on the planet yet the world's richest man is not happy with his lot. He has revealed that he wants to drop the title. *"I wish I wasn't (the world's richest man)"* he told an audience in Seattle, *"there is nothing good that comes out of that."* The billionaire executive said that he disliked the attention his wealth attracted. "*You get more visibility as a result of it"* he said. With regards to happiness, he and his wife say, *"For us, happiness isn't materialistic anymore. But trying to help those who need of our resources"*. The steel tycoon and billionaire Lakshmi Mittal, who ranks the fifth richest man in the world according to *Forbes* magazine some years ago, believes, *"Money can't buy you happiness. I truly believe in inner happiness. Even when something goes wrong at work, I try to remain optimistic and happy.*" Imran Khan, the Pakistan Prime Minister and Cricketing legend doesn't seek *"materialistic happiness any more. Yes, when I was younger, then it was my source of happiness. But now, I'm in search of spiritual and emotional happiness."* In his essay for *Time* magazine, author Pankaj Mishra says the pursuit of happiness is about seeking a deeper sense of contentment. He says, *"The highest form of happiness lies in inner freedom rather than the freedom to acquire and consume."*

Looking at the lives of great personalities, we find that happiness does not come from material things. In other words, happiness is not materialistic. It is rather spiritual or emotional. All of them have stressed inner happiness. All these demonstrate that to experience happiness we need to cross the boundary of materialism and ascend the realm of spirituality. Spirituality refers to the inner dimension of a person. It is the sacred dimension where a person is in touch with his deepest values or a Higher Power which directs his life. His deepest values can be God, love, joy, peace, forgiveness, empathy and compassion. When these values become part of a person's life, he/she experiences happiness.

7

A Sanyasin and a Rich Man

"Anything that cause you your peace is too expensive, learn to let it go."
– Nabaneeta Dutta

Once, a sanyasin and a rich man were together on a pilgrimage. As they were on their way, the sanyasin found a highly valuable precious stone on the side of the road amidst some pebbles. The rich man immediately recognised that it was a rare precious stone and it was of immeasurable value. The rich man was filled with jealousy and was making a clandestine plan to possess the precious stone. As he was obsessed with this thought they came by a river that has a lot of crocodiles in it and the sanyasin without least regrets, threw the valuable precious stone into the deep river. At this the rich man was completely shocked, flabbergasted and a bit annoyed shouted at the sanyasin, "Why did you throw away such a valuable stone into the river when people are spending their whole life just to get one? You could have lived a comfortable life for years to come by selling it." But the sanyasin told him, "I hate it because it is this that blinds many people living in this world." "You are a real and absolute fool" said the rich man. "People call me a fool because I don't accumulate wealth. But they are real and absolute fools who accumulate wealth. When you possess nothing, you're truly free" said the Sanyasin.

- *For the enlightened, happiness, joy, and peace are real wealth. But for the unenlightened, gold, silver, and money are real wealth.*

8

Attractions

"He who cannot resist temptation is not a man."

– Horace Mann

The world today is cloyed with enticements - new technologies, gadgets, fashions, ideas and philosophies. All these can easily sweep us away from what we are today and also what we would like to be in the future. They can dissuade us from achieving our set goals. Therefore, living in such attractive and tempting world, we need to differentiate between our needs and wants.

'*Needs*' are necessary and essential for us to live. While '*wants*' are neither necessary nor essential and we can easily live without them. Our inability to differentiate between the two can potentially impede our growth and prosperity. The danger is that if our *wants* become our *needs,* or if free reign is given to our wants, we can never reach that state of fulfillment and contentment. The reason is that human wants are limitless, boundless and inexhaustible. It is, therefore, almost impossible to satiate human wants. For example, it is not possible for a person to fly like a bird in the sky or want to possess all the gold available in the world or change the law of nature. If we want to be happy and peaceful, we need to take control of our wants. To do this, we need to develop a strong will power to say "No" to all the glamorous allurements of this world. All good things in life are not good for all people in the world.

What is good to one may be deleterious to another and vice versa. Ice cream is so delicious and delectable but fatally harmful to a diabetic. Therefore, one needs to cautiously select things which are good for oneself instead of being swayed by the glamour of this world.

When Ulysses was passing by in his ship, the *Island of the Sirens* (sea nymphs), he filled the ears of his seamen with wax, so that, they would not hear the extremely mellifluous song of the mermaids and had himself bound to the mast, so that he would not be tempted to yield to their attractions. Ulysses knew well that many ships and sailors got drown and perished in the *Island of the Sirens* for they could not withstand their dulcifluous songs which has a seductive and impelling attraction.

- *To live a happy and peaceful life, one needs to curb the glamorous attractions of this world.*

9

A Turning Point in the Life of Alfred Nobel

"I think it's very important to have a feedback loop, where you're constantly thinking about what you've done and how you could be doing it better."
– Elon Musk

Alfred Nobel, a Swedish scientist invented dynamite serendipitously. He was making some nitroglycerine, a highly explosive fluid that goes up at the smallest jolt, when some fell out of a flask down towards the floor. But it fell into a box of fine earth powder, called *'Kieselguhr'* (infusorial earth) and it did not go off. Nobel noticed that the fluid soaked into the powder and formed a sort of paste. With great care he lifted some of the paste out and kneaded it into a pellet. Then, he took it outside the laboratory and set it off. It exploded with great force. He had found a safe way of handling nitroglycerine and he called it *dynamite.*

Nobel's invention made him millions of pounds. But it also made warfare much more destructive and in his later years he felt sorry that he invented the dynamite. His conscience was deeply troubled. Added to his guilt-ridden conscience, another incident shocked him. In 1888, Alfred's brother Ludwig died while visiting Cannes and a French newspaper erroneously published *Alfred's obituary*. It condemned him for his invention of dynamite and this said to have brought about his decision to leave a better legacy after his death. The obituary stated *Le marchand de la mort est mort* (The merchant of death is dead) and went on to say, "Dr. Alfred Nobel, who became rich by finding ways to kill more people faster than ever before, died yesterday." Alfred Nobel was disappointed with what he read and concerned with how he would be remembered. On November 27, 1895, at the Swedish-Norwegian Club in Paris, Nobel signed his last will and testament and set aside the bulk of his estate to establish the *Nobel Prizes* to be awarded annually without distinction of nationality. There were to be five, for scientists, authors and workers for peace.

An obituary lampoon became a source of transformation for Alfred Nobel. This was probably for the first time Nobel came to learn the public opinion about him. In fact, it shocked and shook him up from his ignorance. The good thing about him was that he positively accepted the criticism on his invention and began to change himself. As a result, today, we know Nobel as a noble person.

- *Sometimes it is good to pay attention to what people say about us.*

10

Apply

"Knowing is not enough; we must apply. Willing is not enough; we must do." – **Johann Wolfgang von Goethe**

A soap manufacturer, a confirmed atheist was one day perambulating with a preacher of the gospel. The soap manufacturer said, "The gospel you preach has not done much good for there are still scads of wickedness in the world and a lot of wicked people too." He ranted and raved at the preacher with a battery of charges. The preacher made no reply until they passed by a group of children playing with mud. They were making mud pies and throwing at each other. Seizing his opportunity, the preacher said, "Soap has not done much good in the world, I see, for there is still much dirt and many dirty people around." "Oh, well!" said the manufacturer "soap is useful only when it is applied." "Exactly!" said the preacher "So is the same with the Gospel that I preach."

Application belongs to the practical aspect of doing things. A mere word of application without pragmatism is only a mere theory. We are all called to be doers and not mere theorists. We should give action to our thoughts. Our brainwaves should give birth to a brainchild. Our thoughts should have a corresponding visible manifestation; otherwise, it's all effluvium (waste). All our thoughts become useful only when it has a corresponding tangible expression. Translation of thoughts into action is one of the most demanding tasks.

- *Be doers of your words and thinkers of your actions.*

11

Avarice

"Greed is a bottomless pit which exhausts the person in an endless effort to satisfy the need without ever reaching satisfaction."

– Erich Fromm

During the gold rush days in America, one summer afternoon a steamer crowded with passengers, many of them miners from California suddenly struck a submerged wreck as it sped down the Mississippi. In a moment, her deck was a wild confusion. The boats were able to take off only one-fourth of the passengers; the rest divesting themselves of their garments, succeeded in swimming to shore. Immediately, after the last had quitted the vessel, a man appeared on the deck. Seizing a spar, he leapt into the river but instantly sank like a stone. When the body was recovered, it was found that, while the other passengers were escaping, he had been rifling the miners' trunk and round his waist he had fastened bags of gold. In a quarter of an hour he had amassed more than most men do in a life time but he lost himself in an instant. This is what happens when a person is controlled by greed. The Bible says, "What does it profit a man if he gains the whole world but loses his life? Or what can a man give in exchange for his life?" (Mt. 16:26). Greed has no end and anyone who is stung by the sting of avarice, will find himself constantly anxious, restless, and disturbed as to how to earn or make more wealth. He will experience sleepless nights and restless days. Daily earning is not sufficient. He has no time for his family. It is a joyless pursuit. Since, he works and thinks too much and mentally always alert and anxious, this will take a toll on his mental and physical health. Gradually, his health will deteriorate and finally, surrender his precious life before time and what will he do with his accumulated wealth?

- *Beware! Love of wealth is not only evil but lethal to the soul.*

12

Begin Each Day with a Smile

"Waking up in the morning, I smile twenty-four hours are before me. I vow to live fully in each moment and to look at all beings with the eyes of compassion."

–Venerable Thich Nhat Hanh,
A Buddhist Yen master

Each and every day is new, different, unique, and special. As the day dawns, the night has passed. Darkness has ceased and light has come and you can see everything. Open your eyes and look out through your window. You will find that the whole nature is wrapped in peace and tranquility. Now, give a big SMILE at the vast expanse of this beautiful nature. See what beauty lies there. Smile at all that you see - the grass, the dew drops, the trees, the hills, the valleys, the birds, the insects and enjoy each of them and deem that you are also part of them. This is a very lovely morning. Do you enjoy this regular miracle happening every day? If you are a person of fine sensibility, you will be instantly filled with awe and wonder at such surpassing beauty of nature. You know that all these beauty points to someone SUPREME, who is causing these to happen. Turn towards HIM with a smile and say "Thank You, God!"

Now, the whole day is before you. You do not know what fortune or misfortune that will befall you. You don't know what is going to happen. Therefore, take time to reflect on all that you're going to do and surrender them to God, who knows and directs all things. Smile at Him and ask Him to help you to smile at all the things that will come on your way that day. Then, begin your day!

13

Be Humorous

"A sense of humor... is needed armor. Joy in one's heart and some laughter on one's lips is a sign that the person down deep has a pretty good grasp of life." – **Hugh Sidey**

Humour is the kindly amused contemplation of the incongruities of life and their expression. Humour lightens the sad lot of our life. Life is much easier with a sense of humour. It subtracts the seriousness and the weight of suffering in life. Without humour our world would be a much poorer and hard place to live in. A person who finds some humour in every difficult situation always wins.

People like and love a humorous person. He plays a vital part in the general drama of life. He carries with him the medicine of joy and anyone who tastes this medicine is instantly lightened up with mirth and joy. He is a perspicacious person who communicates affectionately the insights he observes in people. He has no enemy for he makes all happy. A humorous person is therefore, a secured person. A truly humorous person is a person who consoles the sad and doubles the joy of those who are happy. He gently fools others and allows others also to fool him. This is a sign of maturity. A person who does not allow others to fool him or when fooled easily gets provoked or irritated is a sign of immaturity and non-acceptance of oneself! A person who does not accept himself is suffering from a low self-esteem or inferiority complex and will find hard to enjoy life. No amount of validation can cure such deficiency. They are allergic to jokes and fun that are related to them.

There is a German saying, *"Humor ist, wenn man trotzdemlacht"* (loosely translated as Humour means to laugh in the face of mishap). This is the favourite answer of Germans when asked for a definition. It is a way of coping with unfortunate events or tough realities of life. Otto Julius Bierbaum used this German explanation by declaring, *"Humour means the skill to face the imperfection of the world, its everyday challenges and inevitable failures with cheerful calmness."* Close to the first definition of humour, *"Humor ist, wenn man weglacht"* (Humour is when you laugh away). This is the best way to live a happy, cheerful and buoyant life. We need to learn to laugh away with our problems of life. When we make a mistake, laugh away instead of regretting but learn a lesson from it. When somebody creates a problem for you, laugh away instead of reacting to it and find positive way to deal with it. There are so many things to laugh away with in life and if we can master this skill of "laughing away", we can live a happy, peaceful and frolicsome life.

- *Being humorous is one of the best ways to live a happy life.*

14

Be Open to Change!

"A human being will not change his personality pattern when all is said and done unless he is forced to do so by his own suffering. Advice, persuasion requests from the outside will effect only temporary change in the cloak of the personality.... The human ego is a recalcitrant and stubborn affair; it lights off disturbance for it very much fears the profound insecurity that comes when its style of life is shaken."
– Rollo May

Positive change is vital to positive living. Positive change needs to be valued because it leads to a variety of opportunities that makes life meaningful. Change is a necessary part of human unfolding. Regarding change, it has been said, *"What doesn't bend breaks"*. This age old adage tells us the need to be resilient and flexible and avoid rigidity and die-hardism. Rigidity against change can be destructive and detrimental to one's growth and development. So, we need to be open to change. Dawn Demers (2019) writes, *"We should be open to change. But that is not always so easy. We are creatures of habit and our sense of self is rooted in our beliefs and values. However, being open to change doesn't mean losing our sense of self or giving up our values. It just means being flexible and able to adapt to life's ever changing situations and circumstances."*

Being open to change doesn't mean we give in to anything that is new. This may be a naive understanding of change. Being open to change means I am willing to examine my core beliefs and values against the new ones and after having thoroughly and critically analyzed, I have come to know which holds true. Now, after having examined, suppose, I choose the new belief or value, I will certainly be happy and confident because I have updated my set of beliefs and values and this will help me to live a better and more fulfilling life. On the hand, after having scrutinized the new ones, I have decided to hold on to my old set of beliefs and values, it means that they are still relevant and authentic. In such case, I reaffirm my beliefs and values. This will give me the affirmation that the knowledge I hold about "myself" is true. 'Who am I?' is defined by the beliefs and values that I hold deeply in my life. This is the way, we must be open to change. We don't simply change because the world is changing. We change because we need to be better than before so that we are able and competent to adapt to the ever changing environment that will help us in living a meaningful life. We need to change because adaptation is necessary for a better life.

Without 'change' life remains static and non-effervescent. Those who want to live a life of dynamism, determination, ambition and aspiration can't live a fixed and static life. Therefore, change is a must in order to live a motivated and purposeful life. Wanting to change itself is the first step to change. Change as we know is not as easy as riding a roller-coaster. It is difficult to change all of a sudden after years of cultural, social, and religious conditioning. The way we think, speak and act are the result of conditioning and genetic coding. This process of conditioning does not produce the best version of what we ought to be. There are many grey areas and black spots in our lives that need to be worked upon in order to make ourselves better. As relational beings living in the society, we need to change. If everyone thinks and acts according to their individual conditioning without an iota of flexibility, there will be conflicts, incompatibility, differences, and quarrels. If every person thinks that the way he or she thinks, and behaves is the right way, it will surely invite dissention and reaction. Every person views the reality from their own perspective and seldom view from the other person's perspective. Conflict takes place when both are unwilling to view from the each other's perspective and both stick to their guns. People don't change as long as they feel OK. They are likely to change when they feel they are not OK. Therefore, it is always advantageous going through problems in life. This will help us to assess ourselves better and change for the better. The problem with most people is that they need a change but they're not even aware that they need a change. The people around them see their need to change but they themselves are ignorant about it. Such people often have problems in relating with others. Since, we are social beings, we need to live up to the basic and normal ethical expectations of people around us. This does not mean that others dictate me in everything I do, say or think. No! As others expect certain normal and basic moral ways of thinking, speaking and behaving, I also expect others to do the same. This is all about basic and normal human expectations that will smoothen interaction in the society. In short, there are certain basic ethical norms that every individual is expected to adopt in normal circumstances. These are basic rules that facilitate human interaction such as: being polite in words, giving way for the other, not jumping queues, following traffic rules, no smoking in public places, helping a stranger in need and so on. Most of the time, I expect the other person to behave well. I see that the mistake is always with the other. Wanting a change for the other person is not going to change them. Therefore, change has to begin from me. I need to change the way I perceive the inadequacies of others. Changing the way I look at can change the object I look at. Wayne Dyer says, *"If you change the way you look at things, the things you look at change"*. Let us remember that as I expect a change in the other person, I must also know that others expect at least some basic change in me too. Therefore, there is mutuality of expectation. If there is reciprocation in our expectations, it will be beautiful indeed and we will find that life is interesting and enjoyable. Since, no one is perfect, you and I cannot say that "The way I think, speak and behave is perfect". If the presupposition, "No one is perfect" is true, then, we can easily conclude the truth that as you are not perfect; so am I! Therefore, if no one is perfect we need to be open to CHANGE. Change is a necessary condition for constructing a better and improved version of ourselves.

- *Flexibility is one of the best ways to sail smoothly in life.*

15

Be a Conqueror!

"He who conquers others is strong. He who conquers himself is mighty."
– Lao-tzu

Every person is called to be a conqueror. All of our history pages are filled with myriads of superb conquerors. Their names are indelibly imprinted on the pages of history. Some of them are like Asoka, Alexander the Great, and Napoleon Bonaparte etc. but, most of the conquerors were busy conquering and killing others. They had immense physical power to trounce and send shock waves to their enemies. But most of the conquerors' common *Achilles' heel* was that they were not able to conquer themselves. So, to conquer oneself is the toughest battle that a person can ever fight. One who conquers himself conquers everything. There is a double mission to be accomplished by every person:

- The mission to conquer oneself
- The mission to conquer others

Edmund Hillary after he made to the summit of Mount Everest with his co-climber Tenzing Norgay said, *"It is not the mountain we conquer but ourselves"*. There is a scintillating personality who stands out in the Indian history who accomplished this double mission. He is none other than the noble King Asoka. He was an aggressive and truculent conqueror. The famous Kalinga War paved the way for the conquest of his SELF. As a result of the terrible consequence of this war, Asoka's attitude underwent a *volte face*. The bloodshed he caused at Kalinga made him shed tears of conversion. The sight of numerous corpses strewn across the battlefield made his heart wrenched. The battleground looked like a graveyard with bodies of not just soldiers but men, women and children. He saw young children crying over the bodies of their dead parents, women crying over the bodies of their dead husbands, mothers crying over the loss of their children. This made him heartbroken and he made a pledge to never fight a battle again. He then altered his policy from *Dig Vijay* (conquest of territory) to *Dil Vijay* (conquest of the heart). His singular aim now was to conquer his own heart and the hearts of others. From now, he began waging battle in the moral sphere. In order to accomplish this campaign, he embraced Buddhism. He was so inspired by the teachings of the Buddhist monks and philosophies that he used his status to impart this knowledge all over the world. He is credited to be the first Emperor to make a serious attempt at developing Buddhist policies. Plato, the ancient Greek philosopher said, *"The first and best victory is to conquer self. To be conquered by self is, of all things, the most shameful and objectionable"*.

- *The bravest of conquerors is one who conquers himself.*

16

Be Sympathetic!

"Don't be in such a hurry to condemn a person because he doesn't do what you do, or think as you think. There was a time when you didn't know what you know today." **– Malcolm X**

When Swami Vivekananda was a small boy, his father told him the following: *"How can you understand the great misery of human life? When you will realise the depths of human suffering, you will sympathize with these unfortunate creatures who try to forget their sorrows even though only for a short while, in the oblivion created by intoxicants."* This advice had a great impact on the life of Swami Vivekananda. It is a sublime duty of every existential person to be charitable and sympathetic towards others. It is the sad, the distressed, the weak, the abandoned, the unloved and the rejected that need sympathy. Sympathy is a soothing balm that will greatly reduce their sufferings. Whenever and wherever, sympathy is actualized, there will always be an ineffable sweetness and peace for both the giver and the given.

Sympathy is *a loving sensitivity towards others*. It is derived from the Greek prefix "syn" or "sym" which means together or joint and the root word "pathy" which means to feel. It literally means *to feel together*. In other words sympathy simply means a fellow-feeling towards another person. It is the ability to understand other's sufferings and feel sorry for their plight. Its aim is to lighten the lot of the other person's pain and knows no bounds. Sadly, many people have sympathy that is parochialistic. Parochialistic sympathy means that one is sympathetic towards a selected few or group of people. Such person categorizes people into those who deserve and those who do not based on nepotistic evaluation. Such classification based on parochialism and nepotism would expose one's uncharacteristic and uncharitable mindset. Truly speaking, it needs more courage and strength to reach out to the non-deserving than those deserving. Let us take an example of how a person of parochialistic sympathy who possesses a moral superiority complex treats an alcoholic on seeing him:

First of all, he shows a great surprise and abomination.

Secondly, he condemns and judges him.

Thirdly, he sympathizes with the family members and NOT WITH THE ALCOHOLIC.

Such an attitude exhibits an average superficial knowledge of the human person and human situation. The boozer needs more sympathy. He does not deserve sympathy certainly for he has abandoned his family responsibility but even though he does not deserve, he is in real need of sympathy. Our sympathy must cross the boundary of those who deserve and reach out to those who do not deserve like the alcoholic, the drug addict, the streetwalker and other *personae non grata* of the society. They have become what they have become, not because they want to be but circumstances have forced them. I don't think, each of these people basically wanted to become criminals, thieves, drunkards, drug addicts or streetwalkers in life. The environment and circumstances have compelled them to be in such state. Therefore, we look at them through the lens of sympathy and compassion. A prudish or a 'holier-than-thou' attitude will not serve and transform the pariah of the society. Is it not wonderful to see the sympathetic attitude of the authentic man of Palestine, Jesus Christ, who told the woman caught in adultery, "Neither do I condemn you" The Jewish leaders condemned her. According to their law, she must die by lapidation but Jesus did not condemn her. Jesus was never condemnative but ever sympathetic and compassionate. His sympathy reached out mainly to the outcasts or the *personae non grata* who were deemed 'unfit' to be part of the conventional society.

- *It pays a great price to be sympathetic towards those who do not deserve; yet, are indeed in need.*

17

Being at Rest

"The body benefits from movement, and the mind benefits from stillness." **– Sakyong Mipham**

A burglar ransacked the house of a very rich man and borne away with the gold that he had earned all his life. The rich man quickly summoned his neighbours and made a hot chase after the thief. Finally, they came to a thick forest where they came by an old ascetic rapt in meditative reverie. They asked him whether he had seen a man passing that way. "Who is he and why do you look for him?" replied the ascetic. The rich man said, "He is a thief who has stolen all my gold and we are trying to catch him". To this the ascetic said, "You, mundane people, spend all your energy in futile causes like chasing after a thief. Which is better - to run after a material gold that can be stolen or an immortal peace which can never be taken away?" They all said, "Immortal peace! Immortal peace!" "Unless you stop your motion, you will never know what peace is!" said the ascetic.

When we want to find a treasure, we move from one place to another like the rich man and his followers. But if one wants to find an immortal peace, one has to stop moving and one should be at rest like the ascetic. Reflection and meditation are the best tools for attaining and maintaining peace. Meditation becomes possible when a person ceases his or her locomotion. In motion, there is disturbance and distraction. In a state of motion, seeking peace is only chasing after the wind. To find peace, one must stop the physical motion as well as the immanent activities. Greater is the quelling of the interior motion. All motions should come to a halt. When all motions stop, a person reaches the state of being at rest. This state of being at rest is the state of no activity but simply peace. It is a state of no desire, no disturbance, no distraction, no fear etc. You are simply THERE.

18

Be Prepared!

"Spectacular achievement is always preceded by spectacular preparation."
– Robert H. Schuller

SCOUTING has been a great creation but greater still was the mind that created it. His full name is Sir. Robert Stevenson Smith Baden Powell. He is known to the world affectionately as B.P., the very motto of the Scouts "BE PREPARED" is in fact the expansion of B.P's own initials. It means under any circumstances - peace or war, life or death, "Be Prepared!"

Grammatically, the word "prepare" is a portmanteau. It consists of the Latin word "pre" which means "before" and the second word "pare" according to Cassell's Latin Dictionary means "to supply or furnish." Therefore, the word "prepare" in essence means to make it or to furnish or supply the things necessary before you do it. Preparation is a *conditio sine qua non* for successful and fruitful living. Randy Pausch in his book *The Last Lecture* speaks about preparation thus: *"Another way to be prepared is to think negatively. Yes, I'm a great optimist, but, when trying to make decision, I often think of the worst case scenario. I call it 'the eaten by wolves factor.' If I do something, what's the most terrible thing that could happen? Would I be eaten by wolves? One thing that makes it possible to be an optimist, is if you have a contingency plan for when all hell breaks loose. There are a lot of things I don't worry about, because I have a plan in place if they do."* During the period of preparation, we need to anticipate that the worst will happen in the real events of life. In short, prepare for the worst and that will make the preparation intense and the more intense the preparation, the more confidence one gains and the more confidence one gains, the higher the probability of success. It is good to keep in mind 'eaten by the wolves' factor' during the preparation and this can be greatly motivating. We don't prepare to fail but we prepare to meet the worst. Benjamin Franklin's pithy advice runs thus: *"By failing to prepare, you are preparing to fail."*

Doris Kearns Goodwin's book *Team of Rivals* speaks about the importance of Abraham Lincoln's methodical preparation. The book says, *"Before speaking against the Nebraska Act, Lincoln spent many hours in the State Library, studying present and past Congressional Debates so that he could reach back into the stream of American history and tell a clear, reasoned, and compelling tale. He would express no opinion on anything, Herndon (Lincoln's law partner) observed, until he knew his subject "inside and outside, upside and downside."* A student who does not prepare for his examination will eventually fail. So is the person who does not prepare for his life examination. Preparation is a hard and painstaking process. A prepared person is always a ready person. Many people have sunk into abysmal frustration because they have failed to learn the art of preparing themselves. The hardest realities of life can be faced boldly without shuddering and even happily with satisfaction if one is prepared to meet them. Preparation is the variable that must be earned and honed to become and remain a winner in any sphere of life. Preparation is a seed that must be sown on a daily basis. It certainly takes time and hard labour but the reward is sure. But if you prepare today and expect the result instantly, then you can't claim success. Success comes only after a long period of perseverance, discipline, commitment, dedication, and hard work. This is the reason why successful people are minority in history because the majority of people give up on the way. They do not possess the qualities that make a person successful. Bill Gates didn't become a billionaire overnight and so too Warren Buffet and others. Those winners of Olympics did not become champions in a month or a year. It is the result of years of consistent hard work that has made them to ascend the podium as champions. Therefore, if we are people with big dreams in life, we need to prepare seriously and intensely which will certainly take us to the summit. We need to prepare and be ready any time so that we can grab opportunities easily. When Woodrow Wilson the twenty eighth president of the United States was apprised of the nearness of his death he said, “Ready.”

- *Semper paratus! (Always ready).*

19

Bodhisattvas

The Mahayana sect of Buddhism produces a very beautiful and benevolent saints known as *Bodhisattvas*. They are noble persons in the past ages who trod the path of the Buddha and became eligible to attain Buddha-hood. But they stopped at the bodhisattva stage and did not take the final step of entering into the *Nirvanic* stage due to compassion for the suffering humanity. In other words, after having attained Nirvana, these benevolent saints voluntarily delayed their Nirvanic bliss and return back to help those who were struggling to attain liberation on earth. They are also known as compassionate celestial beings.

There are two concepts of the bodhis: *Tatha-gata* and *Tatha-agata*. *Tatha-gata* means *gone thus, in that way*. While, *Tatha-agata* means *come thus, in that way*. *Tatha-gata* means one who has thus gone in realisation from *samsara* (rebirth) to *nirvana* and *Tatha-agata* means one who thus has come from *nirvana* to *samsara* to work for the liberation of all sentient beings. *Tatha-gata* is the one who has realised *samsara* and without delaying enter into *nirvana*. Whereas, *Tatha-agatha* is the one who has realised *samsara* and instead of entering immediately and enjoying his *Nirvana* delays or postpones his *Nirvanic* happiness and comes back to help other beings who are struggling to achieve *nirvana*. *Bodhisatvas* can be called as *Tatha-agatha*.

- *The bodhisattvas are compassionate beings who have only one passion - to attend to the needs of others.*

20

Can't You Live Alone?

"To be yourself in a world that is constantly trying to make you something else is the greatest accomplishment."

– Ralph Waldo Emerson

A person who is afraid to live alone, seeks refuge and security in a group or company. Such person lives in "WE" and hates to live alone. He is afraid of being alone and takes a cozy refuge in "WE". He finds consolation, joy and security in the group. He is at the *beck and call* of the group. He becomes a means for the group and operates on the group's diktat. "WE" becomes his master and his "self" becomes a slave. This is potentially dangerous, for one's dignity and identity is sacrificed on the altar of the group. Such person's dignity and identity becomes the property of the group. He is a mere tool in the collective hands of the group. Such person is no longer free. He is in chains. The weakness of such people is that they will never know 'who they are'. '*What he is' has become 'what the group is'*. He has imbibed the collective identity of the group. He is no longer "I" but "WE". Such people are a lost identity and become chaotic personalities. They are mere living automatons with remote control. Once their identity is gone, their existential meaning is also lost. The most pathetic thing about such people is that they will never know:

- Who they are?
- Why are they here on earth?

- Where is their life moving to?
- What is the meaning of their life?

If as a human person, you are not able to answer these basic existential questions to some extent at least, then you do not understand what life is and you can't live a meaningful life. A person who can live ALONE without feeling lonely is great indeed. He maintains his unique identity and dignity wherever or whatever situation he may be. He is the master of himself and does not allow any foreign ego to intrude upon his affairs. He is capable of managing his own affairs. He is able to stand alone and conduct himself well, even when he is in a group. Collectivism does not affect him. But he affects the group or society. He has command over the group and not the obverse. This type of people gradually metamorphoses into LEADERS. Here, "I" directs "WE"; the singular leads the plural for "I" is capable of leading "WE". "WE" is at the beck and call of the "I". This is how great leaders and personalities are born!

21

Capability Brown

"If we did all the things, we are capable of, we would literally astound ourselves." **– Thomas A. Edison**

Lancet Brown popularly known as Capability Brown was an English landscape architect who changed the natural face of England. He started his life as a gardener. He designed over 170 parks, many of which survive to our day. He was nicknamed "Capability" because he would tell his clients that their property had "capability" for improvement. He saw boundless possibilities in landscapes. He developed a remarkable natural flair for landscape architecture and worked his way up until he was requested by the nobility of England to design the landscaping of their magnificent ornate country residences. He later became a gardener to the king as well. He was so widely involved in his profession that when he was invited to visit Ireland, he responded that he couldn't go because, "I have not finished England yet". His achievements were so wide that he was called, "Nature's second husband".

His famous saying: "It has capabilities, my Lord". He found possibilities in landscapes. As human persons, our task is to see possibilities in people and the things around us. When we meet someone, we should be able to say that *"This person has capabilities"*. Most people don't see capability but incapability. There is tremendous possibility in man and nature. There are vast areas yet to be explored and discovered. Let us be capable of seeing capabilities in nature and in people. Let us not limit them by saying, "good for nothing", "you will never be able" or "you cannot". This is how we destroy people's capabilities. There are limitless capabilities in and around us. Let us look at them with optimistic eyes, ready to explore and transform them.

- *Those who are capable make others capable and vice versa.*

22

Competition

"There is competition, but it is used in a good way. It is positive to want to go first, provided the intention is to pave the way for others, make their path easier, help them, or show the way. Competition is negative when we wish to defeat others, to bring them down in order to lift ourselves up." – **Dalai Lama**

There is a small town located in the southern hill tracts of Manipur, India. The unique feature of this town is that it has many Christian denominational churches. On a bright Sunday morning, a stranger was passing through that town. As he approached the town, he heard many churches' bells peeling forth simultaneously and producing a very melodious and devotional sound. Hearing the sound of the different churches' bells and seeing the beautiful structures of the different churches, the stranger's religious sense was evoked. As he was admiration-filled, he accosted one of the townsmen and said, "Certainly, God is living in your town for there are so many beautiful churches and the melodious choruses that are wafting from the churches are clear signs of God's presence". "What you have seen is completely different from what the reality is", said the townsman, "Here we are living in great tension, intolerance and division. The beautiful churches and the sounds of the churches' bells and the music and the chanting are nothing but the result of a cut-throat competition", said the townsman.

The above story tells us that competition can cause tension, intolerance and division. Even matters related to religion which are meant to be holy can turn into a ruthless competition. Therefore, we need to understand that there are two types of competition - positive and negative. Positive competition is a competition where you put your best effort in order to make yourself better than what you are now. It is about creating the best version of yourself. It is a process of constructing and re-constructing your 'self', trying your best to make yourself better on a daily basis. Here, you compete with yourself. While, negative competition is a competition in which you invest all your efforts in order to defeat another person. The aim of negative competition is to defeat and put down the other person. This kind of competition is harmful. When you give in to this kind of competition, it becomes fatal to yourself because you can't defeat everyone all the time. There will be always somebody who does better than you. When you can't win, despondency, humiliation and discouragement will bog you down. So, having a negatively competitive mind can lead to self-destruction. If you don't check such tendency on time; it is going to harm you more than the person you compete with.

- *Never compete and compare yourself with others, it doesn't build but destroys.*

23

Consciousness: Key to Full Living

"What can a man best do with his life....? Transform into consciousness, an experience as broad as possible."

– Andre Georges Malraux,

A French author, critic, revolutionist and statesman

It is a wonder that "you are"

It is a wonder that "you can act"

And a wonder still is "the way you act"

The way you act or how you act is a real wonder because it shows who you are. The way you act affects your surrounding or environment. It affects others. The way you affect others can be in two ways: destructive or constructive. It can either be a miracle or massacre. The way you act has both the power to transform and to destroy. We know how or the way Hitler and Mother Teresa acted; one destroys and the other transforms. The positive way of affecting others is the greatest miracle that a conscious life can generate. There are two ways in which one can affect those around them - Positive Affect and Negative Affect. Elizabeth Scott (2020) defines *Positive Affect* as a person's "*propensity to experience positive emotions and interact with others and with life's challenges in a positive way. Conversely, Negative Affect involves experiencing the world in a more negative way, feeling negative emotions and more negativity in relationships and surroundings.*" Therefore, if one wants to have a positive impact on others, one needs to cultivate the positive affect in life. Developing a *negative affect* would be harmful. One needs to reduce or eliminate the *negative affect* in one's life. The first step towards cultivating the *positive affect* and reducing the *negative affect* is to become aware of or conscious of both - how they affect our thoughts, words and actions. Then, choose the *positive affect* and increase its quality. Allowing the positive affect to take charge of one's life would augment one's influence on the surroundings. The quality of life increases as our consciousness grows. Consciousness helps one to become aware of and see oneself clearly where one needs to change and improve.

Life must be transformed into limitless boundary. The higher your consciousness, the deeper will be your life experience. Consciousness should be manifested in one's thought, word and deed. A life transformed into consciousness will seldom err. Errors litter the space of our life due to lack of consciousness. Consciousness is therefore, the key to full living. A person can never live fully without being conscious of his life.

24

True Leadership is Crossing One's Boundaries

"An individual has not started living until he can rise above the narrow confines of his individualistic concerns to the broader concerns of all humanity." **– Martin Luther King Jr.**

What are 'boundaries'?

Boundaries are man-made social constructs like tribe, clan, caste, community, culture, politics, religion and other social groups. People like to operate and function within the ambience of these social constructs because they give them security. There is a strong cohesion founded on the principle: *"Same is safe and different is dangerous"*. People easily trust when they find somebody who looks similar to them. Suppose you meet a person of your same race or language or culture, at once, you trust them easily more than people who belong to a different race, language or culture. People who look like me is safe because I have been experiencing such similar people in life and I know them. This is called cultural conditioning. This is how people are made to feel safe within the same tribe, clan, race, community, caste, creed, political party and other social groups. If somebody who is different from them or an outsider or a stranger is found within the same group, he/she is looked at with suspicion and threat. This is because they have never experienced such kind of people earlier.

Yuval Noah Harari in his *New York Times* bestseller, "*Sapiens: A Brief History of Humankind*" mentions about how these *boundaries* are constructed. He uses the term "*shared myths*" by which these *boundaries* are constructed. Every tribe, clan, caste, creed, community and other social groups had leaders who created 'myths' (stories about their common origin, common song, common dance, common language, common beliefs, common custom, common traditions etc.) and convinced people and made them believe in these myths and finally bound them together. These "myths" are passed on from one generation to the next through oral tradition. So, the succeeding generations continue to believe in these myths. These "shared myths" are the binding force that maintains their cohesion. That is why there is a strong emotion attached to these myths. These myths give each member of the group an identity. The members, therefore, will not give up easily but defend these 'myths' at all cost. This is called patriotism, tribalism, clannism or casteism etc. Another reason why these artificially invented social constructs came into existence was to fight against the forces of Natural Selection. Charles Darwin spoke about *Natural Selection* (the survival of the fittest). Natural selection opines that nature selects only the strongest. Example, when a pig gives birth to ten piglets, the strongest one will get more of mother's milk than others because it can outfight its counterparts and that makes it to grow faster, stronger and gradually the strongest. It has enough strength to fight against the rest. While the weak ones which are not able to fight it out to get enough milk will perish gradually. This same process takes place among human beings. In primitive times, the survival principle was "*might is right*". In a community, the strongest person ruled the rest and anybody who was against him would be eliminated instantly. The strongest person controlled the rest with brute force and in the process, he would become unbearable to the rest. So, all the weaker ones who could not fight him back now joins together and killed the strongest one. The unity of the weak was the strategy used in order to survive. This group formation took place in order to fight against the fittest (strongest) so that all got chance to survive including the weak. This was how the formation of tribes, clans, communities, castes, and other social groups took place. All the weak human beings came together to fight against the powerful and stronger ones. If the weak ones remained single, then, they remained weak and could be eliminated but when they were united, they became a strong force and could easily defeat the strongest one. This was how tribes, clans, castes, politics and other social groups came into existence. Its aim is for survival and this was the only way the weak could survive and preserve themselves and their species. This is how the powerful and the strong were defeated in history. This is how artificially invented social boundaries emerged.

These artificially invented social constructs are so ingrained in every human person that all their thoughts, words and actions are all guided by the group's values (ethos/shared myths). I find my identity in them. When somebody ask me: To which tribe do you belong? I effortlessly respond that I belong to such and such tribe or community. So, when I tell my tribe, I get identified. My identity becomes clear for the person who asked me. My identity explains me. Without my tribe I have nowhere to belong to or I become a nonentity. Now, to detach from this is to divest yourself of your identity and it is a very painful thing to do. Example, it is difficult to leave my tribe, my culture, my language, my community, my family completely but if I want to serve humanity (like Mother Teresa or as a an honest social or political leader etc.) and work for all, and I would like people to see me as a person for all, then, I need to change my priority. My priority is no longer my tribe, my community, my clan, my religion etc. My priority should be serving people without boundaries.. This means that my service to humanity as social leader, political leader or religious leader is more important than my family, my tribe, my culture, my language, and my community. These are selfless leaders. Since, many of our leaders today, serve their family, their tribe, their community, their clan first, they are not acceptable to all the communities and some even within their own communities are rejected because they further sub-divide their own community into different sub-categories. To find such an authentic leader in our times is as rare as hen's teeth.

In my own parlance, I call these man-made social constructs as *artificially invented social boundaries*. I call it *artificial* because it is man-made. I call it *boundaries* because they limit or restrict the universal expression of my being. In other words, they prevent us from belonging to all. Leaders and people who cannot overcome these boundaries will struggle in serving people of all communities. His love for his family, tribe, clan, culture, community, language, and religion will take precedence and will be reflected in his thoughts, words and actions. Therefore, if one wants to be a leader who wants to serve humanity, the first requirement is to cross one's boundaries. To do this he needs to have *Omnitenent attitude*. The word *omnitenent* is a portmanteau word. '*Omni*' means *all* and '*tenent*' means *containing*. It literally means *'containing all or everything'*. It is an attitude that contains all. This is an attitude *sans* border. It is sometimes unfortunate to hear a very unpalatable and frequent comments like *this leader or person can't think beyond his tribe, clan, family, religion, political party, community, caste and so on.* To cultivate an *Omnitenent Attitude*, one must learn to accept people who are different from oneself and accept them as his own.

What is important in our times is not theoretical crossing of one's boundaries but demonstrated in one's THOUGHTS, WORDS and ACTIONS. One can be so unprejudiced, unbiased, impartial in words but his or her actions can be just the antithesis. This is called hypocrisy. Therefore, the true identity of a person who has gone beyond the boundaries of man-made social constructs is that his thoughts, words and action will always tally and no dichotomy whatsoever. Those who want to serve humanity ought to cross these artificially constructed social boundaries.

- *Those who are bounded by their social boundaries cannot serve humanity.*

25

Death

"Everything comes to an end; therefore, take heart, for we pass from one thing to another until at last we arrive at eternity. Even seeing how things of this world end so quickly ought to console us because the nearer and more quickly are we approaching that end towards which all our activities should tend."

– St. Teresa Margret of the Sacred Heart

Death and decay are part of the Creator's rhythm of life. It is a biological necessity. Since, man is a biological being he is subjected to death. Death is an inescapable reality. The only way to eschew death is by coming to terms with it. Coming to terms with death gives meaning and maturity to our lives. Happy is the one who foresees death and readies his life to meet it. He is a wise person. But, alas! for the man who does not foresee death, he will have a miserable end fraught with regrets and guilt. Most of the people are afraid to meet death because they are not ready. But a few people in history have accepted death with great joy. One such was Ludwig Wittgenstein, a reputed Austrian-British linguistic philosopher. In April 27, 1951, he was taken violently ill. When his doctor informed him that the end had come, he said, *"Good!"* His last words before he lost consciousness were, *"Tell them I've had a wonderful life"*. He died on April 29, 1951". What a beautiful closure of life! Even the richest man with all his wealth and money cannot have such a wonderful closing of life. A wonderful life always has a wonderful death. Here is a wonderful story about death:

Once, a sick man turned to his doctor as he was preparing to leave the examination room and said, "Doctor, I am afraid to die. Tell me what lies on the other side." Very quietly, the doctor said, "I don't know." "You don't know? You're a Christian man and don't know what's on the other side?" the man said. The doctor was holding the handle of the door and on the other side came a sound of scratching and whining. As he opened the door, the doctor's pet dog sprang into the room and leapt on him with an eager show of gladness. Turning to the patient, the doctor said, "Did you notice my dog? He's never been in this room before. He didn't know what was inside. He knew nothing except that his master was here. And when the door opened, he sprang in – without fear or any other emotion except joy, longing and ecstasy at meeting his master. I know little of what is on the other side of death. But I do know one thing... I know my Master is there and that is enough. I don't care about anything else that may or may not be there."

Man is destined for immortality but through mortality. Man is both mortal and immortal. The material body is mortal while the soul or spirit is immortal. Man is immortal because God has animated him with the spark of immortality. Because of this immortality, death is not the end but the beginning of a new life.

Ovid, the ancient Roman poet said in his poem *"Metamorphoses"* thus: *"Omnia mutatur nihil interit"* (Everything changes, nothing is lost). At death, we are not going to be lost but change. St. Paul in the New Testament has said the same thing, *"I will tell you a mystery. Not all of us will die, but we will all be changed"* (I Corinth 15:51). At, death, what is going to happen is not death but change. Scientifically, it is also proven that nothing will be lost in the universe. All material things will finally change or reduce into atoms. All material bodies will finally turn into atomic particles. When it turns into particles we can't see and therefore we conclude that it is lost. In reality, it is not lost but it has changed its form. As a human being our bodies at death will be transformed (changed) into particles. As the body is buried in the ground, it will decay and turn into particles and make the mud fertile again which will in turn give life to the nearby plants. So, it is not only the soul that is immortal but the body too is immortal. The body has now changed its form and function. We can further explain the reality of death through the metaphor of the Hydrologic Cycle which we all have studied in Geography. When rain comes, the ground is wet, ponds and puddles are filled with water. The next day, as the Sun comes up and with its heat, all the waters in the ponds and puddles get gradually dried up. Now, is the water lost? The water is not lost but has changed its form. Through the process of evaporation, the water which is in a liquid form changes into vapours which is made up of tiny molecules and these molecules are so tiny and light that the wind or air carries them up into the atmosphere. And in the atmosphere, through the process of condensation i.e., these small molecules or tiny particles now join together and form tiny droplets. As the size of the droplets increase, it becomes too heavy to remain in the atmosphere and finally they fall as rain. This is called *precipitation*. So, what we have learnt from the process of evaporation, condensation and precipitation is that water changes its form but it is certainly not lost. The water from the ponds and puddles have disappeared but it is certainly not lost. We can no longer see with our naked eyes. Since, we are not able to see doesn't mean it is lost. But it is up there in the atmosphere and it has only taken different form and shape. This is exactly how death is. That is why, many ancient seers, philosophers and thinkers understood that death is not disappearance but it is a change from one form to another. Life does not evanesce at death but is transformed into a different form.

People who had a happy death in history are those who love and serve God and their fellow human beings. In doing this, they found satisfaction and fulfillment. This is a path to happy death. History has proven that those who love God and their fellow human beings always had a happy death. When Rev. Christopher P. Gadsen, an American clergyman died in 1805, raising his arms to heaven he said, *"I am reaching towards my inheritance"*. James, the Apostle of Jesus Christ and brother of John was crucified in 43 A.D. Kissing his fellow martyr, he said, *"Peace be to thee brother..."* William Ellery Channing, the Father of American Unitarianism said before he died in 1842, *"You need not be anxious concerning tonight. It will be very quiet and peaceful with me"*. Malcolm Muggeridge says, *"I look forward to death with a colossal joy"*. These are some of the people who serve God and their fellow human beings who had a happy death. Even Voltaire, a French revolutionary thinker and a confirmed atheist on his death-bed was attended by a priest who was hoping for his conversion. Voltaire said, *"In the name of God, let me die in peace"*. Socrates once said, *"Death may be of the greatest of all human blessings."* The Guru Granth (p. 579) says, *"Listen, people of the world, dying is not an evil, provided one knows how to die; Blessed is the death of heroic men if they meet it in an approved cause."*

On the other hand, some people died with great perturbation within them. An example is Karl Marx, a German political theorist, who died in 1883. His housekeeper asked him if he had a last message to the world.... He answered, *"Go on, and get out! Last words are for fools who haven't said enough"*. Here are some of the best circumstances in which one can die nobly:

- While serving God.
- While serving others.
- While doing one's duty.

26

Defeatism is an Obnoxious Incapacitator

"Those who give cannot gain victory. It's not victory that is so important, but the fighting spirit. Even if you fail, I think even just the attitude of not giving up is beautiful in itself."

– Lee Min ho

One of the worst feelings that can bog a person down in life is the *feeling of being defeated*. This makes a person incapable of trying again. It sucks up one's energy and enthusiasm. Many people in this world live a life of defeatism. Before they take part in the competition, they have already felt that they won't succeed. Their self-talk is all about, "I think I will not win; I am not that good". Mentally, they have given up. If you are mentally defeated, it is not difficult for your opponent to defeat you in any competition. One can remain mentally invincible even when one is defeated. Can I not win a person who has defeated me? Never quit! I can and you can! What is important is an attitudinal victory! Defeatism is an obnoxious incapacitator. Never allow it to control you. Never allow yourself to be defeated at least before you try. The path of the people who succeed in life are strewn with a concatenation of failures. But they have accepted failures as stepping stones.

In life, things turn out to be in topsy-turvy for those who meet with an accident or ailing with cancer or for people who feel there is no treatment for their disease and left with nothing other than counting the last few days of their life. Believe that you can win against all odds. Rise up to your occasion and make the most out of your living. So, have you been just diagnosed with cancer or have you just lost your eye-sight or a limb in a major vehicle accident? Or have you just been told that you can't live a normal life-style because of your dreaded disease? Understand and accept the fact that nothing can be changed but at least tell yourself that you can change your perception and win against all odds. Know that there are many broken hearts like you, suffering, dependent and getting prone to sympathies of people day after day. Wake up! No, you don't need an injection of adrenaline to walk on your feet; just a NEVER SAY DIE attitude will suffice in order to turn things around. This is the attitude of those who win. They are never defeated even when they fail or lose. Feel that you have to lead a normal life even after knowing that you cannot. You have to tell your story to the human race and to the people ailing with their respective drawbacks and earning their daily sympathy and disappointment. Help your fellow beings, encourage them to live more, remember the trauma you have experienced, absorb it from those ailing in a similar fashion like you. Don't you know Lance Armstrong? He was the seven times *Tour de France* champion. He was diagnosed with testicular cancer in 1996. Only with minute chemotherapy, his ability to fight back and faith gave him the confidence to combat the disease and today he is a living example of one who survived cancer. Indeed, he said, "*Cancer is the best thing that could have ever happened to me.*" He also established the *Yellow Ribbon Cancer Foundation* in the heart of United States helping thousands of people each year.

It is good to learn from the extra-ordinary efforts of ordinary people. You can be an inspiration to all those waiting for an angel to come to embrace them, absorb all their pains and sorrows. Let you be the one, who makes a difference.

Understand the depth and severity of your problem. Think what is achievable within your limits to bring a smile at least on the face of one person, brooding on a life-threatening illness.

Try to live for others and *never give an opportunity to people trying to show some sort of sympathy towards you.* Always remember, 'when the going gets tough, the tough gets going'. This will perpetually help you to fight against all obstacles. As long as possible, make it a point that you are never going to be physically dependent on somebody. You don't need mental support as you are a tough nut to crack. Whenever, you feel lonely, speak and converse with the nature and share your grief and sorrow as the Romantic poet William Wordsworth found consolation and healing in the lap of nature. If nature can calm down and console, it can also offer you her warmest bosom. You need to just connect.

- *Be tough and never accept mental defeat!*

27

Differences in Gifts

Even if one were to perambulate every nook and corner of the world, one would not find a single person who knows everything or who can do everything. Somebody accused God saying that his creation is imperfect, illogical and irrational. The reason why he came to such conclusion was because of the uneven distribution of gifts and wealth among humans. He says that a person who is good at sports has no idea about music and a person who is good at music has no clue about sports or a person who is perfect in oration does not know anything about painting and so on. Biological and anatomical differences like colour (dark, white and yellow), height (short, medium and tall), temperament (sanguine, choleric, melancholic, phlegmatic) etc. are signs of irrational logic. Moreover, some persons are more gifted than others as they possess more gifts or talents than others. This is all the more an enigma. Why some are more gifted than others and some people practically have no outstanding talents at all? We see this unjust disparity of distribution of gifts. This is the view of quite many people in the world.

Let us then, look at from the divine perspective. The differences in the distribution of gifts exhibit the creative ingenuity of God. I see God's wisdom because if a person is given all the talents and gifts, he will not need anyone else in the world. Such person can become supercilious and conceited. We interact and relate with one another because you have what I don't have and I have what you don't have. Human beings fulfill their needs in relationship. The cleverest and the most talented reached such a height of perfection because many people have share what they have with them. Sharing is possible only when we interact and relate with one another. There is always the role "the other" in the blossoming of every person's gift or talent. It is by sharing that we grow. If all stop sharing starting from God, human beings will have nothing including life. We live because of the generosity of God. I grow because of you and you grow because of me. We are given different gifts and talents so that we may share with one another. Gifts are given to me so that I may also share with others. This is the purpose of God sharing his gifts with human beings.

We go to the other person when we need something – emotional, physical, material, psychological or intellectual. In many areas of our lives - to survive and develop, we need the support and help of others. Human relationship continues because of the unequal distribution of gifts and talents by God. Thank God, for His method is illogically logical and irrationally rational!

- *Remember always that you're what you're because of the contribution of many people.*

28

Difference Between Existence and Essence

"Existence without essence is stressful."
– Brian Christian

Existence is the ability of a being to interact with physical or mental reality. *Existence* is the capacity of a being to express itself in the visible and phenomenal sphere. *Existence* refers to outer quality, while, *Essence* is the inner quality. Existence is about the way a person lives his life in the concrete phenomenological world. It is a world where one interacts with another and the universe. All human beings have the same physical structure but differ in their 'essence' (inner quality). It is this 'essence' that makes each human person unique. *Essence* can be defined as "*the basic nature of an entity that determines its shape, its activity, its defining characteristics and possibilities of its everyday life*". It sets the ground rules for actions and purpose that an object can or can't do. This is why most philosophers believe *essence precedes existence.* The basic nature is the inner quality which consists of an individual's values, motives, and purpose that determine the meaning of his existence. It is the inner quality that directs the person.

Each one behaves according to their essence. The interior quality will determine one's external quality. It means one's essence will effect one's existence. The Bible says, "*For out of the abundance of the heart the mouth speaks"* (Mt. 12:34). This means that the inner quality determines the outer quality. A person's core values will find its expression through his activities. So, if a person's essence is stuffed with positive values, his existence will manifest those positive values. But if a person's essence consists of negative values, then, his existence will exhibit negativism. The Bible also says, *"The good person out of the good treasure of the heart produces good and the evil person out of evil treasure produces evil..."*

What is important is the formation of our inner quality. One needs to cultivate values, positive intention and purpose which consists of the inner quality. One needs to be clear of the constituents of one's essence. If one's 'essence' is positive, one's existence will blossom and if one's essence is negative, one's existence will be destructive and baneful. And if one's essence is ambivalent, one's existence will be obscure, misty, and ambiguous.

- *Take care of what makes your essence for it affects your existence.*

29

Differentiate Between Persons and Things

"The most important things in life aren't things."
- Anthony J. D'Angelo

Human beings are persons who are closely related to you and me. I must treat them the way I would like them to treat me. I must do to them the way I would like them do to me. I must speak to them the way I would like them speak to me and I must speak about them the way I would like them to speak about me. I must feel about them the way I would like them to feel about me. I must think of them the way I would like them to think of me. This is the way to understand and treat every human person. Every human being is to be treated as a person with dignity. This is the highest respect that can be accorded to them. Unfortunately, there are human beings who treat their fellow human beings not as persons but objects (commodities - use and throw). This kind of human beings do not know the value of human persons. They manipulate and use human beings without any compunction for their own gain.

The Dalai Lama says, *"People were created to be loved. Things were created to be used. The reason why the world is in chaos is because things are being loved and people are being used"*. What is happening today is that things are more loved, respected and valued than human beings. Human beings are viewed as objects which can be used as long as one wants and discarded when they are no longer needed or useful. I have come across this story in one of my WhatsApp messages. It was so transforming. The story goes thus:

> *While the father was polishing his new car, his four-year-old son picked up a stone and scratched on the side of the car. In his anger, the father slapped the child so hard on his face that the child's eyes began to bleed. At the hospital the child became blind and said, "Dad when will I get all right?" the father felt so sorry and went back to the car and kicked it many times. He then sat and looked at the place where the child scratched and his son had written: "DAD I LOVE YOU".*

This story tells us that the man valued his vehicle more than his son at that particular moment. The man soon realized his misplacement of the hierarchy of values in his life but it was too late and had to regret deeply. Today, persons are treated according to their usefulness. Some people love, respect and show great concern for others as long as they are useful, advantageous and lucrative. They also respect a person according to their qualification and status in the society. To establish relationship with them would mean possessing high status, wealth and high qualification. I don't mean that one should not establish relationship with them. But to establish relationship with the sole motive of getting benefits would be a mockery of a human person. This type of people doesn't bother others who are not useful, advantageous and from whom no gain can be elicited. This kind of treatment reduces a human person to a consumerist being or utilitarian being. It is an insult to the person. This is the basest form of treating a human being.

- *Let us always prefer persons to things. When we lose things, we lose nothing and when we lose a person we lose forever. If you love things more than person, one day you will deeply regret.*

30

Distinguish Between a Person and His Deeds

It is wise to learn and know who a person is!
It is wiser to learn and know who a person is and how he acts
It is wisest to learn and know who a person is and how he acts and to be able to distinguish between the TWO.

However, bad a person may be, he is still our fellow human being. James Kirkup in his poem *No Men Are Foreign*, preaches that all human beings all over the world are our own brothers and sisters. A person may be bad, cruel, uncultured and not worthy of being loved, yet he is still a human person. His personhood (dignity) has not evanesced. However, we have the propensity to judge a person by his deeds and not by what he is. We go from the deeds and conclude that he is such and such person. Many of us take delight in this kind of half-baked incongruous inference. But, the authentic perception about a person may be to find out *who really, he is*. To know this, we need to proceed from the person to his deeds and not *vice versa*. To understand a person, we need to follow the philosophical principle of *"Essence precedes existence"*. Every person is made in the IMAGE of GOD (imago Dei). This is who he or she is. This is the original identity of a human person. He or she may become bad due to situation, circumstances, events, environment or bad influences and so on. We cannot blame a person completely for what he or she has become. There is always an element of other-ness and situations in the process of becoming.

So, we should be able to distinguish the person and his deeds. It will be a naive understanding to identify a person with his deeds. By this, I don't deny that a person and his deeds are completely dichotomized. Surely, the doer effects the deeds. From this vantage point, there is a relationship between the two. At the same time, there is also a visible dichotomy existing between the two. Most people feel deep regrets and compunction after having done a particular action which results in an inner soliloquy: "*Why did I do that or I should not have done that*". St. Paul of Tarsus in the New Testament says, "*I do not understand my own actions. For I do not do what I want, but I do the very thing I hate*" *(Rom 7:15).* All these show that there is a certain discrepancy and chasm that exist between the doer and his deeds. Therefore, the wisest way to learn, know and understand a person is to distinguish between the person and his deeds.

- *If you know the background of every person including a criminal, you will always sympathize with them. You will judge a person until you truly know him/her.*

31

Distinguish Between Noise and Sound

"A seed grows with no sound but a tree falls with huge noise. Destruction has noise, but creation is quiet. This is the power of silence... Grow silently." – **Unknown**

Noise is an indistinct sound. It is a sound that is cacophonous, clangorous, noisy boisterous and disturbing. On the other hand, sound is distinct and it is pleasing and soothing to the ear. When a group of birds like the Nightingale, the Skylark, the Cookoo and the Thrush sing together at the same time, they only produce a noise. Here, one cannot distinguish which is the sound of which bird. But when each of them goes solo, it produces a sound which is so mellifluous and dulcet. Here, one can immediately recognize the sounds of each bird. This is not a noise but a distinct and melodious sound.

In every person, there is a presence of noise and sound. Noise disturbs him and sound soothes him and lifts his spirit. A sound person is one who is at ease with the sound that is within him. While, a noisy person is one who is disturbed by the noise within. There is disorder, confusion and restlessness within that person. It is good to check now and then, whether my inside is filled with noise or sound. If your inside is always filled with noise, you will never hear sound for where there is noise, sound cannot be heard. Therefore, you need to turn down or put off the volume of the noise in order to hear and know what sound is! Why we need to pay attention to sound is because it conveys message. Sound always carries message. Sound has a positive connotation as it is audible, distinctive, relevant and definitive. It has positive effect on health too. While, noise is an unpleasant sound that causes disturbance. Noise carries a negative connotation as it is irrelevant and incomprehensible. It has negative effect on health like hearing loss and hypertension.

A person may be filled with sound but if he doesn't listen to the sound within himself, it is meaningless. A sound becomes meaningful only when a person listens to. When you begin to listen, you will be able to know what kind of sound it is! A person who likes to listen to sound must by all means put off the noise within. Once the noise stops within you, then, that will be the starting point for ascending into the sphere of SILENCE. In order to hear and know what sound is, one needs to ascend into this realm of silence. Once a person enters into this sphere of Silence, he will begin to hear and recognize different sounds. Here, one will start hearing the sound of love, compassion, joy, peace, pain, struggle, suffering etc. One will be able to hear even the sound of the miseries of mankind as Wordsworth in his poem *"Tinttern Abbey"* writes that he could hear the "*sad music of humanity*". The peak experience of this sphere is that one will be able to hear and recognize the sound of the *silent steps of God*. The whole world is filled with the sound of GOD, who is the source of all sounds. We are called to listen to the sound of God.

- *Sound begins to resonate when there is a interior silence.*

32

Dobson's Five Principles of Discipline

One of the most helpful, practical and down-to-earth books on discipline is James Dobson's "*Dare to Discipline*". Dr. Dobson has taught pediatrics at the University of Southern California School of Medicine in Los Angeles. "I am thoroughly convinced that the proper control of children can be found in a reasonable commonsense philosophy where five key elements are involved" he says. They are as follows:

(a) Develop respect for the parents. "If you want your child to accept your values when he reaches his teen years, then you must be worthy of his respect during the younger days" Dobson advises.

(b) To recognize that communication often improves after punishment.

(c) Control without nagging.

(d) Do not saturate the child with excessive materialism. He feels that temporary deprivation heightens appreciation. Excessive materialism diminishes the thrill of receiving.

(e) Avoid extremes in control and love.

33

Do Not Expect a Reward for a Good Deed

A man who does great good and talks not of it, is truly great. But the man who has accomplished a small good and magnifies it in his talks is only a worthless and pompous gasbag.

It is a universal propensity to seek a reward for a good deed. Yet a person's true greatness is seen when he or she is able to transcend this universal tendency. People generally follow the principle "*quid pro quo*" (give and take), which implies that if I give you something, you must also reciprocate with something. It is a principle of reciprocation. So, the general proclivity is that if I do something for you, at least you must thank me for it. I have heard this repeated hackneyed remark of some people that runs thus: "He is such an ungrateful wretch. I did everything for him but didn't care even to say just a word of thanks". This type of people helps others in order to receive a reward. Jesus in the Bible says, *"Let your right hand not know what your left hand is doing"*. Here, Jesus is urging not to keep record of the good that we do. He wants us to go beyond the level of seeking recognition in whatever good we do. Expecting a recognition for a good done is an average man's way of looking at life. But those who are able to go transcend the level of recognition are living a morally higher level of life. For them, it doesn't matter whether people are grateful to them or not. They are no longer affected whether they are thanked or not. They are able to maintain their equanimity.

Ingratitude has generated many estrangements in relationships for the giver feels dissatisfied with the response of the receiver. In such situation, when a person's good deed is not reciprocated, he must learn to maintain his equanimity. Equanimity should be maintained whether I am recognised or not for the good I have done. When I am recognised I should feel a just and legitimate happiness and not elated about it. I must be able to do the same even when I am not recognised or at least thanked. This is equanimity. Any discrepancy in this situation will perturb one's *equanimity.* When equanimity is not maintained, a person will feel extremely elated for being recognised or appreciated and extremely depressed when he/she is not recognised or appreciated. There is an equanimity breakdown. When there is equanimity breakdown, it can take a person to either extremes. The Guru Granth (p. 219) speaks about an equanimous person thus,

"Such a man is a sage with equipoise;
That man is an enlightened Sage
Who in happiness and suffering,
Remains poised with equanimity
Who in glory and shame
Feels just the same,
As well from sorrow and pain; Who cares not for praise?
Nor even for blame
But seeks the state of Nirvana."

It is true that every person needs at least some amount of recognition and appreciation. It is just and legitimate to appreciate and recognise people for the good they have done. At the same time, every person has the power and strength to transcend the levels of recognition and appreciation and reach the realm of equanimity. It is hard and painful to go beyond these levels but it is not impossibility.

In doing any good, I must not have even an iota of a lurking expectation for a reward of any sort. If one has entertained such an unalterable psychological beggary, then such person is bound to get dissatisfied in life for "things don't usually happen according to our expectation". If you are a person constantly looking for a reward, what will happen to you, when your expectations go flat? It takes time for a good deed to gain recognition. Sometimes you may not live to see the fruits of your good deeds in your life time. That is why there are many unsung heroes. Some people received recognition posthumously. Your good deeds may go unnoticed and unrecognised. Nevertheless, it is sure to live on and inspire somebody around you who will share the inspiration with others. A good deed always lives and inspires on. Your life may be like a mist that appears for a little while and then vanishes; yet, your good deeds will live and inspire others and lead them on.

- *Do all that you can for others. Expect nothing in return. When you do this, deem that you're doing to yourself and take no pride. Then, even the 'smallest action will appear gigantic'. This will keep you on and you will find that life is interesting.*

34

Do not Add, Be Proportionate!

Once a student was severely upbraided just for a peccadillo (small mistake) by his teacher. The student sharply reacted against the words of his teacher. Another soft and understanding teacher interrupted and told the student, "Jack! Why do you react so much? After all, he is your teacher". "Sir! I am reacting not to him but the additions he attached to my mistake. He awarded me a severe castigation for a peccadillo" said Jack.

There are many people who suffer unjustly because we often attach additions to their mistakes and often magnify to a frazzle. Exaggeration always hurts. We don't convey their mistake as it is but as it seems to us. To convey the mistake of others as it is without any addition is to convey the truth and to convey this truth sympathetically to the mistake-maker is to correct or to lift that person from his mistake. We must redeem a person from his mistake and not destroy him. Every person will react sharply when additions are attached to their mistake. A person will surely listen and accept his mistake if conveyed with sympathetic proportionality. Most people will react if he is given a severe castigation for a minor offence because it is not proportionate. Even a child knows when he is treated unjustly or unproportionately. Anything that is not proportionate is an offence against fairness. Unproportionate treatment is another name for inequity.

- *When punishment is unproportionate to the offence committed, it always hurts.*

35

Don't Be Merely Optimistic but Stoical

"When you come out of the storm you won't be the same person that walked in. That's what the storm is all about."

– Haruki Murakami

Bertrand Russel writes in his autobiography, *"I am amazed at the number of people who are wretched almost beyond endurance. And the world seems to me quite dreadful; the unhappiness of most people is very great and I often wonder how they all endure it."* Life is not an easy sailing. At times, it is difficult to pull on and endure the concomitant sufferings life brings. Often people surrender when they feel that it is beyond their capacity to endure. Yet, there are tough people who can stretch beyond the limit. These are tough people who do tough things in life. Any amount of affliction doesn't not bog them down. The more they face life's problems, the tougher they become.

People often compliment us to be optimistic in the face of suffering but being optimistic alone is not enough to face tough things in life. To be optimistic is just to have a positive attitude towards the tough situations one is going through. It is not enough to have a positive attitude towards problems and sufferings but a tough mental strength is required. *Be optimistic!* is a compliment that is peripheral and simplistic. I think the better compliment should be: *Be stoical!* The first compliment is about treating the situation with conventional protocol that comes spontaneously without any effort; while, the second compliment *"Be stoical!"* contains an element of audacity and boldness in facing the situation. It is better to be STOICAL than just be optimistic! Being stoical makes a person daring, firm, and heroic. It is a fearless approach to situations of life. A stoic never gives up in any situation, however tough it may be. The noblest part of being a stoic is to die in the fight rather than give up. People who possess a huge reservoir of mental toughness are never defeated mentally even when they have lost the fight. Ultimately, this leads them to see life heroically and finally, at the end of their lives, they are able to sing their song of victory:

> *"I am so happy and satisfied that I fought a good fight"*. But what we have to know about stoics is that they are not foolhardy and impetuous. They weigh, measure, calculate, study and analyze their thoughts and actions. After they have identified things of value, then they don't compromise. They pursue such things fearlessly and courageously. Ryan Holiday in his book *The Daily Stoic* writes a short and beautiful prayer of a stoic, *"God, grant me the serenity to accept the things I cannot change, the courage to change the things I can, and the wisdom to know the difference."* Stoics are the ones who know themselves better than others. Ryan Holiday also describes a stoic as one who tells himself, *"I will keep constant watch over myself and - most usefully - will put each day up for review. For this is what makes us evil - that none of us looks back upon only that which we are about to do. And yet our plans for the future descend from the past."* **- Seneca, Moral Letters, 88.2**

A school boy one day asked J. Krishnamurti after a talk in his school: "Sir, are you happy?" Krishnamurti answered at once, *"I don't know. I haven't thought about it. But if I begin to think about it, I'll definitely feel unhappy."* Happiness is how you feel and how you feel is mainly comes from your attitude and your attitude must be either optimistic or stoical. If your attitude is pessimistic, then, certainly, you'll be a grumbler finding fault with everything around you and everybody knows that grumblers are seldom happy. Happiness is the result of fighting stoically the toughest battles of life.

- *Being stoical is crossing the boundary of mere optimism and fighting valiantly the hard battles of life.*

36

Dr. Ambedkar: A Victim of Untouchability

"My fight against UNTOUCHABILITY is a fight against the impure in humanity." – **M.K. Gandhi**

Dr. Ambedkar was a multi-dimensional man of genius, a brilliant academician, a popular attorney, an erudite scholar, a great legal luminary, a powerful writer, a journalist, a constitutional pundit, emancipator of the rights and liberties of the dumb, downtrodden and suppressed people. Social justice was the mission of his life. Such an illustrious personality had to suffer great injustice because he belonged to an untouchable Hindu community. Let us see some of the painful incidents he suffered in his life as an untouchable:

- Bhim (young Ambedkar) as a school boy belonging to a low caste was made to sit outside the class and no teacher would ask him any question or correct his notes for fear of contamination. Whenever the teacher wanted to punish the child of lower caste, he would throw things at him from a distance. One day he felt thirsty and reach for the common glass to drink water, the other students shouted, "Stop! Don't touch that glass? It will get polluted. They complained to the teacher." "Bhim, you must not touch the common drinking glass again," said the teacher angrily. "Now sit down and cup your hands."

The teacher poured water into his hands keeping as much distance as he could.

- Another occasion, he went to receive a hairdo. After sometime, the barber realised that he is cutting the hair of an untouchable. "How dare you come to me for a haircut!" shouted the barber. "Get out at once! You have defiled my instruments." Feeling so humiliated Bhim made his way home with half of his hair cut. People pointed and laughed at him.
- Once on his way back from school it started raining heavily. He huddled against the wall of a house for the lashing to stop. Suddenly, a window opened and the owner of the house peeped out. She recognised Bhim as an untouchable. She rushed out of the house with a stick, "Why are you leaning against my wall? You have contaminated it," she cried in rage. "Now go away before I beat you black and blue with a stick." And then, she pushed the child violently. Bhim fell down and hurt himself badly. Sobbing and bleeding he ran back home in the rain. How could the little boy forget?
- One day the teacher asked him question and said, "Bhim, come to the blackboard and explain it." Bhim walked up to the blackboard, but before he could reach it, there was a stampede. "What is the matter?" shouted the teacher angrily. "Sir, we want to pick up our lunchboxes which are lying behind the blackboard. Bhim is an untouchable. His shadow will contaminate our food," they said.
- Bhim and his brother were once travelling in a bullock-cart to reach home. The cart-man asked their caste. "We are Mahars," replied Bhim truthfully. "Mahars! Screamed the cart-man, outraged, "how dare you sit in my cart and pollute it! Get off at once!" His brother said, "We'll pay you double the fare." "Very well said the cart-man grumpily. "My day is ruined. First thing in the morning

I'll have to go home and purify myself, my animals and my cart."

- Once the owner of the guest house called him and said, "Is it true that you are an untouchable?" "Yes" replied Ambedkar. "Get out at once from my guest house," said the Parsi owner angrily. "Give me a few days to find some other accommodation," said Ambedkar. "Durwans" shouted the owner in rage, "throw this man out with his belongings."
- One day his loving teacher called him and said, "I would like to give you my name. May I change your name from Ambavade to Ambedkar?" "Thank you, Sir, I am honoured," said Bhim who was overjoyed this name was an upper caste Hindu surname. His brilliance impressed his Brahmin teacher Sir. Ambedkar. "Bhim bring your book to my desk," said Ambedkar, "I want to show all the children the wonderful work you have done."

  "B...b...but Sir, I am a Mahar. No teacher has ever touched my copy," said he taken aback. "Well," said the teacher, smiling, "What interest me is not your caste but your work." "This boy is extraordinary. He'll go far" the teacher often told himself.
- *When your mind is hijacked by man-made parochial constructs like caste, creed, race, tribe, etc., you are limiting the possibilities of knowing another person.*

37

Ego-Hypersensitivity

"I believe that the largest problem that humanity faces is an ego sensitivity..." – **Ray Dalio**

Our world is full of imperfections. We see people striving after imperfections and not after perfection. Some of the imperfections are manifested in the form of corruption, bribery, red tapism, scams and frauds, cheating, flagrancy, violence, moral profligacy and so on. All these imperfections are used as tools for achieving one's own egoistic ends. There is a blind striving for one's own gain. *Feeding of the Ego* has come to hold the stage. The "I" has gain prominence and the "We" is struggling to survive. Nobody cares about 'We' if 'I', 'the Ego', 'the Single', and 'the Alone' has a cozy existence. Why should 'I', the Single bother about others? I am 'I' and not 'We'. I am content with myself and why should the needs of 'We' bother me. I hate the concept of 'We' because 'We' never satisfy my needs. It is 'I' who feed myself. I was born alone; I struggle alone and I will die alone. No one dares to be with me in all these grimmest situations of my life. This is what I call as Ego-Hypersensitivity.

Due to Ego-hypersensitivity, imperfections are strangely burgeoning every day in our society today. People love to choose to live in the lonesome absurd situation. This is an imperfect microcosm. The individual's ego-hypersensitivity has generated many a suffering in the world. It has caused tears and blood. Arthur Schopenhauer, a hardcore German pessimistic philosopher has rightly pointed out the imperfect situation of human beings when he said, "*Homo homini lupus*" which means "a man is a wolf to another man". It is human beings who have no inhibition or compunction to swallow another human being in order to fatten and preserve his EGO. He has sacrificed his human nature for animalism. The ego-hypersensitivity has turned him into a devouring monster. Unless and until the ego-hypersensitivity is overcome, it is difficult to predict a pacifistic life in the society. Therefore, every "I" must sacrifice and forego all the unjust and selfish proclivities in order to alleviate the collective sufferings of mankind.

The unguided Ego is potentially dangerous and has the power to eliminate the "WE" from the globe. One of the best examples is Hitler. The untamed ego is a wild beast. On the contrary, if the ego is tamed, the imperfections and the absurd situation can be reduced to a great proportion.

- *Let us learn to let go our ego.*

38

Endurance

"Unless you have courage, a courage that keeps you going, always going, no matter what happens, there is no certainty of success. It is really an endurance race." **– Henry Ford**

A person may be made of a strong and robust physical constitution, yet he may be suffering from deficiency of mental toughness. Physical sturdiness is not the criterion for measuring one's inner strength. Man is measured by the amount of *mental toughness* he can generate in a given task or situation. There is a story of a sparrow and a snare. The sparrow saw the Snare climbing on a big and tall guava tree. The sparrow accosted the Snare, "Where are you going?" the Snare replied, "I am climbing to reach the top of the guava tree and taste its fruit". At this the sparrow began to laugh and mock at the Snare and said, "How foolish you are! There is no fruit on the tree and it is not the season. Above all you are so slow and when will you get to the top." To this the Snare said, "By the time I reach the top there will be fruits". After many months, when the Snare was enjoying the ripe fruits of the tree another bird came and said, "How did you manage to get here?" the Snare said, "I began my journey last year and today I am here enjoying the fruits".

Can you imagine the journey of the Snare? In order to get to the top of the guava tree the Snare had to endure so much of sufferings - the harsh weather, the wind, the rain, the storm, and the heat for months without rest but still didn't give up because it was sure that by the time it reached the top, there would be fruits. The Snare was clear of its dream and never retracted. The Snare didn't see the fruits but it was certain that the fruits will be available in due season. The only thing it has to do was "to make the climb" and it did it.

Dr. Ishwari Prasad, an Indian historian writes about Babur, *"No distress of misfortune could disturb his equanimity and whether on the field of battle or on the edge of precipice in the hilly country he moved forward with a merry heart"*. Life is not a bed of roses. The life of some people is just made of a series of unfortunate concatenation of mishaps and that makes them stronger and tougher to deal with life's problems. Napoleon Bonaparte and his soldiers had to endure the extreme cold and the frostbites in order to cross the Alps which were considered most formidable obstacle in those days.

- *If you want to reap the fruits of life, you must endure.*

39

Enthusiasm

"Every great moment in the annals of history is the triumph of enthusiasm."
- Emerson

It is enthusiasm that makes a person swarm the heights of success. The etymological background of this magic word is the conglomeration of two Greek words - *'en'* meaning *'in'* and *'theos'* meaning *'god'*. Enthusiasm therefore, literally means 'God in us". The enthusiastic person is one who speaks or acts as though he were possessed by God. When you say that he is very active and alive, you only mean he is full of enthusiasm. When we say that such person is fully alive, we only mean that he is full of enthusiasm. It is this magic word that takes a person to the great pinnacle of success and achievements. A person's success depends on the amount of enthusiasm he possesses. The size of the achievement will depend on the amount of enthusiasm a person is able to generate. There was always great enthusiasm behind every great achievement in history, as Emerson's words inscribed on the wall of his private office read: "*Nothing great was ever achieved without enthusiasm*". Dale Carnegie writes, *"A person can accomplish almost anything for which he has unlimited enthusiasm."* He also wrote a booklet called *The Little Known Secret of Success* which deals with enthusiasm. In this book he said that it's not education, it's not connections, and it's not the way you dress. The people who go the farthest in life are excited about something. There is a greater chance of success for a more enthusiastic person than a less enthusiastic person. A person who keeps on blowing the embers of enthusiasm will soon see the miracles generated by it. It was enthusiasm which guided the great orators, geniuses, philosophers, and scientists to scale great heights in the past. Enthusiasm gave birth to numerous inventions and discoveries. It has been an operating force in the past history, the present history and also for the history to come. Cultivate enthusiasm and allow it to unfold itself within you and keep on fanning its flame and you will soon see wonders happening in your life.

Life is an energy. It is how we use this energy that will determine our lives. If we fuel our world with positive energy daily, we can accomplish unimaginable things in life. But if our world lacks energy, we have nothing to take us to the destinations we want to arrive at. Enthusiasm is an energy that has tremendous potential to take us to great heights in life. Therefore, we need to fuel ourselves with it on a daily basis. Enthusiasm is the wondrous fuel that runs the engine of life. It is directly associated with passion. We must find our passion in order to experience enthusiasm. We will never experience enthusiasm by doing what we don't like and this will certainly bring down our level of enthusiasm. Knowing our passion is doing what we like and love and this will generate an overwhelming enthusiasm. Honore de Balzac has given us a great piece for reflection: "*A man dies for the first time, the day he loses his enthusiasm.*" One daily habit we must practice is to IGNITE OUR ENTHUSIASM every day.

- *Without enthusiasm a person is only a living cadaver.*

40

Every Cloud has a Silver Lining

"A pessimist sees the difficulty in every opportunity. An optimist sees the opportunity in every difficulty."

– Sir Winston Churchill

Once there were two persons. One looked up into the sky and saw nothing except only the thick cloud enveloping the whole sky. The other person looked up and to his surprise he not only saw the cloud but also a special lining that decorated the cloud and beautify the sky. The first one is a pessimist and the second an optimist. The pessimist, when beset by problems and pains sees nothing except the problems and pains. In other words, he sees only the thick clouds. He thinks that once he is caught in the web of problems and pain, there is no escape and no solution. He feels that he is irredeemable and therefore not worth trying a solution. He has no hope and allows gloom to encircle him.

On the contrary, the optimist always holds that every problem and pain has its bright side. He perceives that life is beyond problems and pain. He is able to see the things beyond the thick clouds. He is able to rise above problems and pains. He hopes that every problem and pain will pass someday and they can be overcome and that there is a solution. He may not be able to overcome just now or today but he hopes that someday victory will dawn. There was a shoe company which sent out two of its agents to go and assess the prospects of marketing in Africa. When the two agents came back, one of them reported, "Nobody is using shoes in Africa and therefore, it won't be wise to take our shoes and sell there. Since, no one is using shoes, no one will buy." The other person reported, "Since, no one is using shoes, it is very prospective for us to go and sell. No company has gone so far there and sell their shoes. Indeed, we will be the first one. Therefore, the people are going to like our shoes." The first agent is a pessimist and the second, an optimist. The *'optimism'* comes from the Latin word *'optimus'* meaning 'best', which describes about how an optimistic person is always looking for the best in any situation and expecting good things to happen. The term *'pessimism'* derives from the Latin word *'pessimus'* which means 'worst'. Therefore, a pessimistic person is one who is always looking for the worst in any situation and expecting bad thing to happen.

- *Are you a pessimist or an optimist?*

41

Evil: A Means for Good

"Good and Evil are not like Black and White, it's not easy to tell the difference because, I guess they are tainted by each other. Good and Evil are both Grey." – **Unknown**

Thomas Robert Malthus, an English clergyman, economist and moral philosopher, who was famous for his contribution to population studies in his *"First Essays"* says, *"Evil exists in the world not to create despair but activity"*. Evil is a necessary means for good. There is no good without evil. We are able to identify what is good because of the existence of evil. If there is no evil, how do you define good? Because of evil, one is able to have clarity on what is good. Suppose, if there is no darkness, how do you define light. We recognize light because of the existence of darkness. The world is teeming with evil that the good seems to be utterly overshadowed. Nevertheless, the reality that evil exists in the world should not bring us to desperation but active activity. We should insipidly fight against them. The greater the evil, the greater the good awaits to be achieved. The size of the good depends on the size of the evil. The greater evil you defeat the greater good you shall achieve.

Robert Malthus as an influential economist was trying to solve the problem of limited food supply. He saw that the evil of hunger can ravage humanity's survival. Therefore, he came out with his theory known as the "Malthusian theory". This theory explicates that the population grows in a geometrical fashion and food supply grows in an arithmetic progression. Food supply increases at a slower rate than the population. This can result in disequilibrium. If this continues, food supply will be limited in few years. As a parish priest, Robert Malthus saw in his parish and beyond the evil of hunger or limited food supply that was affecting the rural poor of England and many other countries. Because of this he was inspired to take up a research and came out with a theory that could solve the problem. His theory continues to inspire many economists up to our day to bring solution to the problems regarding population and food. So, what we see in the life of Robert Malthus is that evil can be a source of inspiration for people to bring about good. Evil is also an opportunity that has the potential to create good. We must not see evil as evil per se but as a jar containing possibilities to generate good.

42

Faithfulness, Loyalty and Obedience

"Obedience to lawful authority is the foundation of manly character."
– Robert E. Lees

Bhai Lahana who later became Guru Angad Dev was one of the most faithful and loyal disciples of Guru Nanak. The Guru tested him so many times. His pet disciple emerged successful every time that he was tested. Because of his surpassing faithfulness, loyalty and obedience, Guru Nanak chose him as his successor instead of his own son. Here are some of the most interesting incidents through which Guru Nanak tested the faithfulness, loyalty and obedience of BhaiLahana.

- It was a very shivering mid-night and Guru Nanak's disciples and sons of the Guru were relaxing. Guruji yelled that his clothes had become dirty and who would go and wash them? Getting such order at such odd hour and in so trying conditions, all his disciples began to look left and right to parry his call. But BhaiLahana immediately got up and reached the river and washed the soiled clothes, undaunted by the adverse weather.
- One more event of such types took place. Guru Nanak had some grain fields at Khartarpur and also some milch animals. BhaiLahana was responsible for their upkeep. One day it was raining cats and dogs and all the fields

were immersed in water. But the fodder for cattle had exhausted. So, the Guruji ordered, "My animals are hungry as no fodder is left now. One of you, my disciples should go to the fields and get the fodder." At this order everyone became speechless. But BhaiLahana immediately stood up and went.

- In the same manner Guruji asked him to bring salt from Khadoor in biting cold weather as there was no salt left for the Langer (mass-feast). BhaiLahana went there and brought salt carrying sack-load over his head. Many people had come to have food at the Langer.
- Having concern for the people Guru Nanak ordered his disciples and sons to climb atop the *keekar* (babool) tree and shake its branches and feed the people on the sweets that will be showered by the tree by your shaking. Hearing this queer order both the sons were baffled, "How could a tree shower sweets? That too, from a *Babool* tree? Thinking that their father was not normal, both of them quickly slipped away. But BhaiLahana climbed atop and did as told by the Guruji. When he shook the tree, everybody presents there witnessed the unusual sight of that *Babool* tree showering sweet fruits.
- One more such grim test was conducted by the Guruji to ascertain who among his disciples was most devoted to him. Guru Nanak adopted the guise of an insane man and started beating anyone who happened to come before him with a stick to the dismay of all his disciples. Guru left for the woods in the same state. The dogs of the village barked at him. By warding them off with his stick he continued to move ahead. He was being followed by his sons and disciples including Baba Budha and BhaiLahana. The Guru finally reached near a crematorium and stood near a dead body. When his disciples reached near him, Guruji said, "Come...ye all! You must be hungry. Today I'd offer you a delicious

food. Look, how tasty is this dead body? Eat it and satiate your hunger." All his disciples were utterly gobsmacked at this order. What sort of filthy order Guruji was giving? How could any sane man eat a dead body? When none of his disciple was ready to obey his order, Guruji asked BhaiLahana:

"Well, BhaiLahana! Aren't you hungry? Even if you are not hungry, I order you to eat this dead body."

BhaiLahana did not hesitate for a moment and reached near the dead body to obey Guruji's instructions.

"Order me, Guru Dev! From which side I should start devouring the dead body, from the head-side or the feet-side?"

"Begin from the feet side" said Guruji

Surprisingly, when BhaiLahana lifted up the veil over the body, there was no dead body at all.

"Guruji you wanted me to devour the dead body but there is no dead body" exclaimed BhaiLahana.

"BhaiLahana! I was just testing you people's devotion to me and only you emerged successful. Come close into my embrace. Since, you have touched my body *(ang)* you shall henceforth be named as 'ANGAD' (one who touched the body of Guru Nanak).

By that time, Guru Nanak had become quite aged. Three months before his spirit's final coalescence with the supreme Spirit, he officially seated BhaiLahana on the seat of the Guru.

- *Trust is built upon three foundational pillars - faithfulness, loyalty and obedience.*

43

Fifteen Rules for Happy Living

1. Live a simple life and do not be too formalistic. Be temperate in your habits.
2. Live a humble life. People love and respect a humble person.
3. Do not be selfish and egocentric. Learn to give, it is not a loss. We only reap what we have sown.
4. Spend less than you earn. This may be difficult but it pays a big dividend. Keep out of debt. Cultivate frugality, prudence and self-denial. Avoid extravagance.
5. Cultivate the good habit of listening to others. Try to see the other's point of view.
6. Cultivate a grateful heart. Everybody likes to be thanked and complimented for what they have done. Give to people what they deserve. Be generous in your compliments.
7. Be optimistic! Believe that for every problem there is always a solution.
8. Be generous! There is no greater joy in life than the joy that comes from intelligent giving.
9. Be consultative! Any decision that you take always consult people who matter and you will seldom err.
10. Work with right motives. Let your motive be beneficial to all. People will judge your motive by your action. They should not say, "This person is doing only for himself/herself or he/she is partial."

11. Be interested in others! Move your mind from self-centrism to other-centrism. Serve and help others always for this is a sure way to happiness and fulfillment in life.
12. Have a hobby. Nature study, walking, gardening, music, voice culture, foreign language, books, photography, social service, public speaking, travel, authorship and so on are examples. Cultivate an avocation to which you can turn for diversion and relaxation.
13. Live for a day at a time. Make the best use of today for it is all you have. Tomorrow is not in your hand and so forget it and concentrate on the tasks of today. If you do well today, tomorrow will be alright.
14. Have something to achieve in life and work for it without ceasing. Someday when you look back you can tell yourself with a sense of satisfaction, "I did it."
15. Above all these, keep close to God. Ultimately, true and lasting happiness depends on our close alliance with Him.

44

Follow the Mother Bird

"Take action! Wanting is not enough; act upon your goals! If somebody was watching your day-to-day behavior, would they be able to see what you're working towards; what your goals are? If the answer is no, FIX IT!" **– Dr. Steve Maraboli**

A man on his way to his *jhum* field saw little birds in a nest being fed by their mother. The mother bird brought food for its little ones. Seeing this little drama for a few days, whenever he passed by that way, an idea struck him one day and he said to himself, "If God cares for these little birds so much by sending the mother bird, why can't God send food for me who is more worth and valuable than these little birds." So, he started sitting down under the tree waiting to be fed, thinking that God will send somebody to feed him like the little birds. Days passed nobody came to feed him. Finally, he became extremely hungry. As he was wriggling in hunger, he heard a voice, "You fool! Follow the mother bird not the little ones".

- *Some people live a parasitic life because they have no purpose in life.*

45

Frederic Passy: "The Apostle of Peace"

"We must begin to inculcate our children against militarism by educating them in the spirit of pacifism. Our school books glorify war and conceal it's horror. I would teach peace rather than war."

– Albert Einstein

Frederic Passy is known as *"The Apostle of Peace"* – a title he richly earned. The first Nobel Prize for Peace was awarded to him and Henri Dunant in 1901. For 65 years he trod lecture platforms, put pen to paper, pouring out a prolific output from pamphlets to books and with a scholarly acumen used his training in law and economic theory in efforts to track down and destroy the causes of war. The Crimean War and the Loire flood were the two incidents that moved him to question why humanity should be callous and cavalier to suffering in war and yet feel sympathy to that caused by natural disasters? For him this was not an idle question but rather the catalyst which thrust a generally liberal humanitarian into life-long commitment to a *"war against war."* For him, hostilities found nourishment in the acrid brew of competition.

He was a persuasive man. He wrote eloquent pleas in the journal *"Le Temps"* for peace between France and Prussia in their contest over Luxembourg in 1867 and he was widely credited for helping to avert the threatened war. In 1896, he wrote a stunning article published in the "*American Journal of Sociology*", a summary of the many successes of the peace movements. He closed this article saying,

> "*As for myself, I have labored unceasingly in this cause for 30 years and in spite of temporary defeats and mortifications, I have never despaired of ultimate success... the horizon is brightening; deeds have spoken louder than words... It is time to say openly...that the reign of violence is over and the universal conscience demands the rule of justice.*"

- *We need to be peacemakers, not peace preachers.*

46

Genius

"Genius means transcendent capacity of taking trouble first of all."
– Thomas Carlyle

A few men have been born into the world with an exceptional quantum of talents. "Genius" is the word by which they are known. When a genius displays his talent, the witnesses are most often awe-stricken and all agog at the dazzling quality of his abilities. At such moment, people look at the brilliant skills of the genius and forget to look at themselves without realising that they also possess such potential. Finally, they end up with a pathetic soliloquy such as, "Oh, if I could be like him!" or "Oh, I can't be like him!" or "He is born for that." Such people think that a genius is born and they cannot be like them.

A genius is not born but made, largely self-made. Most people have forgotten that a genius in order to perfect his ability or skill and gain immortal renown have **left no stone unturned.** The Latin phrase for "leave no stone unturned" goes *"Omnem movere lapidem"*. This adage originated from an ancient Greek legend. When Xerxes made war on the Greeks and was vanquished at Salamis, he himself escaped and left Mardonius behind to carry on the war in his name. Mardonius also lost the battle at Plataeae and escaped from the battlefield. There was a rumour that Mardonius before escaping had buried an immense treasure in the ground near his tent. Incited by this prospect, Polycrates, a Theban bought that piece of ground. However, when he looked for the treasure long and thoroughly and had made no progress. He consulted the oracle of Delphi, as to how he could find that treasure. Apollo replied in these words "leave no stone unturned". As soon as he had done this, he found, they say, a great hoard of gold. The success of every genius is because they were ready to leave no stone unturned. The meaning of *"leave no stone unturned"*:

- Do everything that is possible in order to achieve something.
- Make every possible effort.
- Search in all possible places.
- Do everything you can to achieve a result.
- Do something carefully and thoroughly, not missing any step.

A genius is one who practices the abovementioned statements rigorously and thoroughly in their lives. He toils and swarms the heights of success in the night while the rest are asleep. A genius is one who attains the touch of perfection in his particular set goal. This perfection is achieved as a result of determination and patient endurance. He is one who is able to withstand unshakably against the weathering wind and sun and storm and rain in varying intensity. He does not spare his energy in order to attain his dream. The more he invests his energy, the more perfect he becomes. Michaelangelo once said, *"The more the marble wastes, the more the statue grows."* A genius is one who gives up everything and do only what matters the most. The more he sacrifices, the more he grows.

A genius is one who aspires and then perspires and finally inspires. He begins with aspiration and willingly goes through the process of perspiration and ultimately, his life becomes an inspiration for others. So, the success formula is:

ASPIRATION (Goal)→PERSPIRATION (Effort)→ INSPIRATION (Success + Legacy)

Only a few people have become geniuses because the majority of the people aspire to accomplish but they do not want to perspire. This is the reason why geniuses are minority in history because only a few are willing to aspire and perspire in life. Listen to the words of Michael Douglas Mallock:

"The tree that never had to fight
For the sun and air and light
That stood out in the open plain
And always got its share of rain
Never became a forest king
But lived and died a scrubby thing.

The man who never had to win his share
Of the sun and sky and light and air
Never became a manly man
But lived and died as he began."

47

Give Your Time to Others

"The greatest gift you can give someone is your TIME because when you give your time, you are giving a portion of your life that you will never get back." **– Unknown**

Martin Buber, an Austrian Jewish and religious existentialist philosopher best known for his philosophy of dialogue, a form of existentialism focused on the distinction between the I-Thou relationship and the I-It relationship. He directed his philosophical speculation towards *"I-Thou"* from *"I-It"*, which focuses peak importance on the human person after a very sad incident. A young man came to Buber's office one day, asking for an iota of time, "I need to see you, Sir" he said. But Buber declined on the ground that he was preparing a paper for delivery at a convention at a later date. That awful night the young man killed himself. His suicide deeply touched Buber and changed him forever. This sad incident awakened him from his ignorant slumber and made him realize the gargantuan importance of interpersonal relationship. Buber deeply regretted that he didn't give his time.

The amount of time you spend on others is as important as the amount of time you spend on yourself. There is a pleasant joy in living for others. Therefore, give and share your time and energy for others. Your love and generosity can be best demonstrated by how much you are available to others. We should be genially approachable, easily accessible and pleasantly available to others without least squiggling. A person who says, "I love you and care for you" but can't make himself available when you're in need, is only a mere eyewash. It is all balderdash for love is always available to its love.

Hieun –Tsang, the most celebrated antique pilgrim to India writes about the good king Harsha. He says, *"He (Harsha) was indefatigable and forgot sleep and food in the discharge of his duties. Again, the day was too short for him.... He was the busiest of man and devoted all his time to promote the welfare of the people"*.

- *Availability is love actualized!*

48

Hero or Zero

"A hero is someone who has given his or her life to something bigger than oneself." **- Joseph Campbell**

Once a boy in a hostel was caught for writing a *billet doux* during study hour by the warden. The warden called him to his office and asked him, "Have not your parents sent you here to study?" "Yes, Sir" replied the boy. "Then why did you waste your time in writing this futile love-letter during study hour?" questioned the warden. "I love the girl" said the boy. With this the warden went berserk and started lashing the boy as he shouted, "You cannot love both the girl and your book at the same time. You must marry either". After a heavy bout of flogging, the boy did not exhibit any sense of pain. The surprised warden angrily asked, "Why are you not crying?" the boy solemnly replied, "I am a Hero".

Today, our society is full of self-styled heroes (self-proclaimed leaders). All want to be hero and nobody wants to be zero. In the process of trying to become hero many have turned into zeroes (achieving nothing). To be a true hero, one has to begin from zero. This is the road to hero-hood as shown by Jesus to his disciples, *"Anyone who wants to become great must be the smallest among you"*. Remember, according to Jesus' principle, zero is the starting point of Hero-hood. This is a proven road to travel! If you want to be great, begin always from zero. In other words, be humble! A person who is proud and egotistical is in fact, barricading himself from the benefits that come from others. When you don't allow people's ideas and skills to flow in to you, you will never learn and improve yourself. People don't like to share what they know and have to a person who is pompous and conceited. Be humble and be open and people will give you even what you don't ask! Only those who learn get enlightened! If you want to be a hero, who wants to accomplish great things in life, you need to start from zero. Any success is largely because of the contribution made by others to the achiever. Therefore, being a humble learner will keep the door open for others to contribute generously to your life.

49

Have I Become?

"To be yourself in a world that is constantly trying to make you something else is the greatest accomplishment."

– Ralph Waldo Emerson

I live in a world which is laden with brokenness caused by misunderstanding, hatred, jealousy, greed and violence. Every turn I take, I only face criticism, deprecation, scoffing, contempt, and derision. This world seems to be so indifferent and cavalier and not even willing to contribute anything positive that would make me grow. I just hate how people around me behave. Due to their obscurantist attitude, they can't see me doing good and getting my 'self' better. I feel alienated but I have no choice. In such a hazy and cloudy world, I have to find the meaning of my life. Therefore, there is an urgent need to construct my "self" and find meaning in my life. I have to take the responsibility of constructing myself and no more self-pity. I have to make myself strong and invincible. So far, I thought the world would help and make me prosper but in course of time, I have found that the world is no longer reliable and can't depend upon anymore. Ultimately, I have learned the greatest lesson of life i.e., build, develop and perfect yourself without depending on anybody. The day I realized that I have to depend wholly on myself that was the day I began to grow. Let the world remain indifferent, apathetic and insouciant, I don't care! I am alright and I can confidently say, "I can manage and regulate my life".

I am not custom-made. I have to constantly make and remake myself. This will lead me to discover the meaning of my life. I will go through the hard process of constructing and reconstructing my 'self' without rest, till *"my 'self'* becomes *"that 'self'"* (that which I want to become). I can make my 'self' what only I alone want to be. So, I am wholly responsible for this task. This is the noblest task of my life and I am ready to pay any price. Jean Paul Sartre conceives a person as *"a being for himself"*. He also says, *"Man is what he makes himself."* Therefore, the art of constructing and reconstructing myself is a sacred duty I have to perform every day; otherwise, I will never *become. Becoming* will lead me *to become* what I want *to become.* Therefore, till I *become*, I will not sit and stare. I know that *becoming* is hard and painful process. *Becoming* is a process of choosing all that will facilitate me to reach *that self.* I have to choose diligently because some of the wrong choices I made in the past brought me regrets and a feeling of guilt and bogged me down. Each day brings a new menu of choices. So, I have to make new and diligent choices every day. Wrong choices can retard my growth and it can cloud my goal.

The goal that I am hoping is to become *that 'self' - the fully developed self,* and when I reach *that 'self'* I will be different from what I am now. The only thing I will experience when I reach there is *the feeling of being fulfilled and satisfied.*

- *The best transformation is self-transformation. It is a waste your time trying to transform others.*

50

How to Deal With Children

"A child is an uncut diamond." **– Austin O' Malley**

Children are the most precious gifts of God entrusted to parents, teachers, elders and the whole society. Children are the future makers of our society. How they are formed will impact the condition of our society tomorrow. Therefore, there is an urgent need to pay attention, so as to how to train and shape them. Children need to experience adequate love, attention and acceptance in the family, school and society. Creating an ambience of love, care, acceptance and attention will make them to grow healthy. Let us see what makes them feel lack of acceptance, love and care and those that build them:

What makes children feel lack of acceptance?

(a) Constantly chiding and criticizing them creates feelings of failure, rejection and inadequacy.

(b) Comparing children with other children makes them feel a lack of acceptance.

(c) Expecting children to achieve their parents' unfulfilled dreams causes them to feel alienated and unaccepted.

(d) Overprotection harms child's growth.

What builds a sense of acceptance?

(a) Recognize children as unique. Never compare them. Comparison destroys.

(b) Help children find satisfaction in achievements.
(c) Let children know you love them, want them and really enjoy them.
(d) Accept children's friends.
(e) Give more attention to the child who is sad or sick or differently-abled among them.
(f) Treat children as persons of worth. They have a very promising future.
(g) Allow children to grow and develop in their own unique way.
(h) Children are not there to fulfill the unfulfilled dreams of the parents. They must be given the freedom to pursue the dreams that they want.

- *Acceptance means loving children whether good or bad, playful or sober, mischievous or obedient, naughty or well-behaved. Acceptance gives them belongingness and belongingness gives them security and security gives them confidence and confidence leads them to live a successful life.*

51

Human Beings are Mistake Makers

"To step aside is human." – **Robert Burns**

Human beings are by nature mistake makers. There is no person who was born perfect. A person who claims to have not committed any mistake is either an angel or God. The Latin phrase *"Humanum est errare"* (to err is human) rightly depicts the authentic nature of human beings. It is human to make mistakes again and again and again. But he is truly wise who consistently persists in his effort to win over his mistakes. It does not matter how many mistakes you have committed. But it matters how many essays (attempts) you have made to overcome your mistakes. One should be made of a sterner stuff and never remain servile or subservient to one's mistakes. Never entertain a defeatist attitude towards mistakes. A person who has a defeatist attitude says, "Oh, I have made a mistake! This only shows that I am only human. It's alright!" Such person recognizes his mistake but chooses to remain in the quagmire of mistake. He is self-complacent with his mistakes. Such person will never climb the ladder of growth in life. Every person has a potential to go beyond his human-ness. It is said, *"Wise people learn from others mistakes and foolish people learn from their mistakes."* Wise people are observant and they learn from the behaviour of other people through sagacious and percipient observation.

Mistakes should teach us. We should draw lessons of life from them. Mistakes are fountain from which flow lessons of life. Mistakes should ennoble us. It should warn us, teach us, show us a new way and above all it should open our eyes, minds and hearts to see a new way of living our lives. The stronger the mistake, the greater should be the lesson drawn. Mistakes should correct and purify us. One who does not draw lesson out of their mistakes is a fool without profit.

- *The difference between the wise and the fool is that wise people never commit the same mistake twice but fools make the same mistake again and again.*

52

Human Beings Are Not Functionaries

"Do not let the roles you play in life make you forget that you are human." **– Roy T. Bennett**

The world today is a fragmented reality. From this fragmentation arises a situation in which human beings are looked upon as *a collection of functionaries* or *an agglomeration of functions*. There is a strong tendency today, to identify a person with his function. A person is known by his function. He is what he does. Examples like, "He is a builder", "She is a singer", "She is a house-wife", "He is a painter", "He is a driver" etc. In all these, the person is forgotten and only their functions are recognized. Builder, singer, house-wife, painter, driver etc. are all the roles/ functions of the persons. Identifying a person with his/her role/ function depersonalizes his/her dignity. It is an insult to their dignity as human beings when we identify a person only with their functions. Human beings become only a functionary role-player. They are being atomized i.e., one atom interacting with another atom but they have no identity. This is a depletion of human value. The human person is divested of his value. When you view a human person from the point of his role/function, you are limiting yourself from understanding the beauty of that person in a wholesome manner. In a society which is hierarchical, you will find that the function of a person is of great importance. If your role is important, you will be treated as an important person, but if your role is insignificant, you will be treated accordingly. In a *hierarchical society*, a person's dignity is determined by the social roles or functions. But in an *equality-based culture*, all the members of the society are treated equally, role or function does not determine a person's dignity.

- *Recognize a person as he or she is and not as what he or she performs (function).*

53

I am Against the Political Mind

"Politicians and diapers should be changed frequently and all for the same reason." – **Jose Maria de Eca de Quieroz**

Osho in his book *Unio Mystica* beautifully illustrates about the political mind. He is deadly against this political mindset which is the greatest weapon of manipulation that is let loose upon the *hoi polloi*. Let us see what he has to say about the *Political Mind*: "The political mind means the cunning mind. The political mind means the murderous, violent mind. The political mind means the mind that is only interested in being in such a position where millions of people's lives are in his hands, this way or that. The politician's mind is the mind of the perfect egoist. I am certainly against the political mind. I would like a world which does not go round and round the political mind. I would like a world which has the *religious quality not the political quality*. At least I would like the political quality of the mind to recede into the background. At the center should be the creative mind. Politics is destructive. But this cannot happen right now. For millions of years politics has been in the center, so this cannot happen right now. A great meditative energy has to be released first. If millions of people become meditators then slowly, the structure of the energy on this earth will change – will start moving from the political mind to the religious mind. I am against the political mind, but I know that this cannot happen right now. It may take thousands of years. The beginning has to happen right now, the seed has to be sown right now and your life will have a flowering. But as far as the whole earth is concerned, it is going to take time".

Osho in the above paragraph describes his perspective on the political mindset. He says that the political mindset has no compunction and guilt after it has committed crimes. It wants to stay only in power. This is a Machiavellian mindset where the end justifies the means. It is an egoistic mindset which puts one's own needs before that of others. It manipulates millions of lives and treat them as mere instruments to get what it wants. This mindset is dangerous and destructive. Osho says that he would like to usher into a world which is dominated by religious quality than political quality. Religious quality and political quality are two opposing values. Religious quality refers to love, joy, peace, compassion, forgiveness, and equanimity. While political quality refers to power struggle, competition, rivalry, opposition and so on. In order to bring about religious quality, one needs to practice meditation (calming of the mind). Once the mind is calm, peace or equanimity will automatically follow. Political mind is a mind that contains power, competition, and rivalry. While, the religious mind is a mind that contains peace, love, joy, truth, compassion, and forgiveness. What is important is which quality, do we put in our minds? If all human beings stack their minds with religious quality, we can create a peaceful world. Once the political mind is changed into religious mind, there will be peace and prosperity in the world. When politicians' political mind gets transformed into religious mind, politics will undergo purgation. But this can be a terribly acclivous task but not impossible. Osho says that this "is going to take time". So, he suggests that "the seed must be sown right now". Therefore, the task at hand is to sow the seeds of religious quality in our minds.

- *All politicians must be guided by political ethics (ethics of process and ethics of policy).*

54

I and YOU Make WE

"I promise to always be there for you... We are a team, you and me... I am on your side, to support you and build you up when you are feeling down. I am here to encourage you and to cheer you, to be your best friend and to love you." **- Karen Kastyla**

How can *WE* exist when I and You are not there? The word *WE* is born as a result of You and I coming together. So, *"You and I"* create *"WE"*. When You are not there, how can *WE be* and when I am not there, how can *WE* exist! Therefore, without You, *WE* cannot live and without me, WE cannot exist. Please, I beg you to come to me or allow me to come to you, so that *WE* can live. If You love me and I love you, *WE* will be very happy indeed! But if You hate me and I hate You, *WE* will disintegrate. Please, don't go away because if you go away, *WE* will stop existing. *WE* don't want to die and so you come to me and I come to you so that *WE* can meet and when *WE* meet, *WE* will be happy because *WE* were looking for each other and *WE* have found.

WE is a collective concept consisting of *You* and *Me*. You and I are two relational subjects that make up the collective concept called *WE*. As long as *WE* (you and I) are able to live together in peace, the concept of *WE* will continue to grow. But if *WE* (you and I) are not able to relate and co-exist together then, the concept of *WE* will have a meaningless existence. So, all human beings are relational beings and there is meaning in living together in unity, and sharing our existence together. When all live together, and support one another, there will be progress and growth. Unity can be fostered only when You and I, the chief components of WE are able to live together. When You and I, love one another, shun hate, WE can live a peaceful and progressive life.

- *Let us give a chance for WE to live.*

55

If You Want to Be Well, Love Yourself First

"To love oneself is the beginning of a life-long romance."

– Oscar Wilde

Our traditional spirituality has been urging us to hate and forget ourselves. This is the point where inner-contradiction, confusion and guilt begins in one's SELF. From this begins the spiritual crisis of a person. We must learn to love and care for ourselves otherwise we will end up hating or being indifferent to ourselves. The Bible says "Love your neighbour as you *love yourself*" (Mk. 12:31). Loving oneself is a commandment and it is not a mere statement of truth or principle. It is an obligation. We must learn to love ourselves. Unless I love myself, how can I love you? A person who hates himself cannot love others. We must love ourselves positively and healthily. How do I love myself? Here are some of the ways you can cultivate to love yourself:

- *Self-acceptance:* I accept myself as I am i.e., I have weaknesses and also strengths. There are some things which I am good at and also not good at. I try my best to be the best I can be. I will try my best to change or rectify my weaknesses and those which I cannot change or rectify, I shall accept them as part of me. This is self-acceptance.

- *Be grateful:* Make an inventory of those things which you are good at (abilities and talents). Express your gratitude for the person that you are. Cultivate appreciation for your strengths and gifts. Also, feel a sense of gratitude that you are alive and well and fully capable of making a difference in your life.
- *Forgive yourself:* You need to learn to forgive yourself if you want to live a free and happy life. Forgiveness sets you free. Regrets and guilt in your life occur as a result of not forgiving yourself. If you have committed mistakes in the past that has caused you to feel guilty and less worthy of yourself, you need to forgive yourself. All make mistakes and therefore, there is no need to beat yourself up for those mistakes. Sometimes, we are so harsh and blame ourselves for failures to achieve or failures to act etc.
- *No self-criticism:* Never berate yourself over a peccadillo. Is there an inner voice that often tells you that you are not good because you are stupid or make mistakes often? Do not believe such voice. Change the inner voice which will tell you that you are not bad, and you can improve; never give up! If you find that you are self-destructive and judgmental, make a conscious effort to stop such negativism. Tell yourself that you are not all bad. From just one good, you can build up the rest.
- *Inject yourself with fun-tonic:* Inject some fun into your life. Life is meant to be enjoyed. Don't take life too seriously at times. If you can think of life in this manner, you automatically relax and quit worrying over things that do not matter. Do not allow birds to build nests on your head. Shirk off all the negative things that come to you and do not allow them to make nests on your head. This can choke your growth and wellbeing.
- *Acknowledge your effort:* Life is not always about winning or coming tops in everything that you do. Many times,

it is the sustained effort that counts. Acknowledge that you have done your best, even if you have failed to produce tangible results. Investing all your energy may not necessarily lead you to success but it will give you the satisfaction that you have done your best. So, be happy that you have put your best effort.

- *Be kind and positive to yourself:* When you begin to think kindly and positively about yourself, the love you have for yourself just grows. Make it a habit to praise yourself everyday as you stand in front of the mirror. Because of such positive thoughts, you naturally undertake empowering actions that support your development. Remind yourself always that your blood type is *Be Positive.*
- *Trust yourself:* Have confidence in your abilities. Know that you have the ability to make important changes for yourself, for as long as you put your heart to it. If you trust yourself, you will be surprised that you can do more than what you think you can do.
- *Be truthful to yourself:* Loving yourself requires you to be truthful about your own feelings. If you are happy, acknowledge the joy. If you are sad, acknowledge the sorrow. When you are truthful about your feelings, you do not try to lie to yourself or seek to bury your negative emotions. Instead, acknowledging what you feel provides a good guide to what your thoughts are.
- *Make positive affirmations daily:* Regularly, pass positive affirmations on yourself. For instance, say this to yourself, "I love and accept myself completely and unconditionally". Tell yourself, "Well done!" over the little success and "Never say die" over your small failures. Practice this exercise every day.
- *Look after your body:* It is important that you strengthen yourself with proper nutrition and regular exercise. Your body is a sacred temple and you should treat it with

respect, love and care. It has been found that the lack of self-love is often the root cause of conditions like eating disorder, obesity, diabetics or even terminal diseases. If your body is not healthy, you can't enjoy life. Sri Ravishankar says, *"Your life partner is your body.... You and your body stay together from birth till death. What you do to your body is your responsibility and that will come back to you. The more you care for your body, the more your body will care for you."* Jim Rohn, an American author and speaker says, *"Take care of your body. It's the only place you have to live"*.

56

Is Your Word Congruent with Your Deed?

"May you live your life as if the maxim of your actions were to become universal law."
– Immanuel Kant

It is your words and deeds that demonstrate who you are. People listen to your words and observe what you do. By this simple methodology, they are able to scan and detect who you are - honest or dishonest, sincere or insincere, selfish or generous and good or bad. We are living in a curious world, where people have the proclivity for nitpicking or pedantic fault-finding. They are curious to know what you think, what you say, and what you do. They are judgmental. They are ready to judge whether you are right or wrong in what you say and what you do. They are ready to misjudge you too. They will never leave you un-judged. Therefore, take care of what you think, what you say and what you do.

So, happy is the person who is honest and errorless in his words and deeds. When people find that your life is errorless and honest, they will begin to trust you. You have become a person with authenticity and integrity. Seeing this authenticity and integrity, people will begin to respect you. There are a few traits by which we can identify people with authenticity and integrity.

- *No hidden agenda:* Authentic people have no hidden agenda in their relationship with others. This means that in any business or a deal, you don't look for your benefit alone. You also look for the benefit of the person whom you deal with. You are sincerely concerned about them and try your best to make them grow as you make yourself grow. In order words, you don't cheat or trick the person you deal with.

- *Their words tally with their deeds:* One of the most visible signs of authentic people is that their words tally with their actions. They act on their words. They follow what they say. If they make a promise to someone, they fulfill it. They live a life of integrity.
- *They are not judgmental:* Authentic people refuse to judge others. There is a difference between making an observation and making a judgment. Noticing somebody coming late for an important meeting is making an observation but thinking that the person is bad because of the late arrival is a judgment. Authentic people never judge others.
- *They are vulnerable:* Authentic people easily trust others because without trust they can't relate with others. Since, they are good to everyone whom they come into contact with, they become vulnerable. People are not all good. One out of ten whom they meet can be a cheat. Authentic people in their goodness, trust people easily which becomes their Achilles' heel. Since, they are authentic, they don't want to mistrust others. This is how many good and authenic people are hoodwinked.
- *Authenticity is an alignment of our thoughts, words and deeds.*

57

It Takes Courage to Be Different

"Courage isn't having the strength to go on - it is going on when you don't have strength." – **Napoleon Bonaparte**

A certain great man of letters is said to have declared on his death-bed that Homer bored him. It was almost the last-hour confession to get rid of the guilt feeling brought on him by a secret disagreement with the judgment of mankind at large. Literarily, people of all generations consider Homer to be the greatest epic poets of all time and so his literary virtues had to be extolled and what is worst in his poems also had to be enjoyed. But this certain man of letters had never succeeded in appreciating Homer. He had repeatedly tried to read *Iliad* and *Odyssey* and they had fallen from his hands. He had kept his disappointment to himself. How could he declare that Homer bored him when all cultured people around him enjoyed his works visibly and proclaimed them to be the best epics ever written by the hand of man? There would definitely have been something wrong with him if he had differed from the universal opinion of literary experts everywhere. Something would be lacking in him if he was not able to appreciate Homer as others did and so he dissembled, nodded his head and at most kept discreetly quiet when others sang the old bard's praises. He saw nothing where others saw marvels. Would his eyes be at fault? No, his eyes were not sick and his literary taste was not wanting; only he was DIFFERENT. And it takes COURAGE TO BE

DIFFERENT in a society that prizes conformity and rewards compliance. So, he kept his opinion to himself, laboured through life under the burden of his concealed rebellion and finally cleared his soul at the last moment with the public announcement: *Homer bores me.* Then, he died in peace.

There are many educated, learned and erudite intellectuals in every society who are not able to express that they have a different way of looking at things. In other words, they have no space to be different. Because being different can cause indifference from the conventional society. Sometimes, being different can be fatally expensive, so it is better to keep one's views under hibernation. The forces that protect and preserve the conventional world-view are so strong that any move to alter or change is looked at with suspicion and threat. They would go the extent of preserving their world-view at any cost. Because of this threat, many seasoned thinkers with great ideas for better society have gone without expressing themselves. We can't blame them for the society adores conformity with conventions and traditions. Anything beyond this causes ostracism and rejection from the society. Today, the greatest regret and pain in our societies is the silence and indifference of intellectual luminaries that are carriers of potentially transforming ideas that can give birth to great change in the society.

- *Being different is not indifference. It is a new way of bringing a change.*

58

Find a Reason to Live

A few years back I came across the following story from a magazine. The story runs thus: A teenage girl was writing from her school hostel to her father who was dying of cancer thus: "I am writing this letter on a subject that is important to me as it is to you, a subject that has been a burden to me and about which I can best express myself in a letter. Life is a struggle and one has to accept the ups and downs of life. That is what you taught me. I now ask that you maintain a positive attitude, for life has to be fought – a life that is important to you and to me. You say you have terminal illness and want to just give up, surrender! Think – what effect does it have on Mamma? You must support her as she does you. Do you realize she prefers to sit by you and look after you, rather than face the fact that you have gone through? She needs you as much as we your children do. We are with you in your suffering and so feel for you; we are your flesh and blood and so empathize deeply with you.

We want you to be with us for long; so, keep up your struggle and hope, if not for yourself at least for Mamma's sake and for the sake of all your loved ones who need you! For me dear Daddy, for me! For soon I will be finishing school and would want you to be there when I get my graduation certificate. What a joy and privilege it would be to present it to you who deserve it the most! You have looked after me, cared for me and provided well for me! All I now want is that you cherish the fruit of your long years of labour and sacrifice."

The father expressed his thoughts as follows:

"My child's letter gave me new hope, new strength, something to struggle and live for. I read the letter again and again; I long to live and see her graduation. That's the strong will I placed myself in." However, the father died barely three weeks before the child received her diploma.

It's lonesomeness with little light,
The terminally ill feels ill at ease;
Deep despair descends and so solace flees,
In his dark night of defeat and past plight!
A touch, a soothing word then gives some strength
Raises hope, a glimmer of light appears,
Bringing in some peace and quiet at length,
Driving away despondency, fears and tears!

In life we need a strong reason to live for. Amidst sufferings, terminal illness, discouragement, depression, and despondency, one can still see a glimpse of hope, if one has a strong reason to live. For those who have no strong reason to live, give up easily. They don't have even an iota of strength to try. Each one of us must discover one strong reason to live for in this life. Strong reason engenders strong determination to pull on and endure the toughest struggles of life.

- *If one has no reason, one is wasting one's life. When one wastes his life, he will in turn affect somebody else to waste their life too.*

59

Know to Whom You Are Preaching

Once, a Guru sent out a band of enthusiastic disciples on a preaching mission. The young disciples went with great gusto from place to place teaching simple people with noble doctrines. On their return, one of the disciples complained that he could not convince a certain man. He said, "I preached to him with great enthusiasm but all in vain." The Guru asked him, "Did you know the man?" "No" replied the disciple. Again, the Guru asked, "Did you know his state?" the disciple said, "No." "You are an infant preacher" said the Guru, "now go and learn the man and I will tell you what you should do". After having learned the man, the disciple came back and told his Guru that the man was poor and had not eaten for days. The Guru told him, "Take some food and give him. After that you preach." The disciple did as he was told and came back successful in his mission.

- *To teach and preach effectively one needs to know to whom one is preaching or teaching. The reverse is a fiasco.*

60

Learn to Accept Other's Viewpoint

"Nothing is more dangerous than a dogmatic worldview - nothing more constraining, more blinding to innovation, more destructive of openness to novelty." **– Stephen Jay Gould**

We live in a world of subjective truth. Everyone claims that his idea or what he thinks is the truth for him. It is the subjective-self that verifies the truth of one's claims. This is what we called subjective relativism i.e., what is true for me, is true for me, though it may not be true for you. Truth is relative. The individual has become the ultimate arbitrator of morality. This is the genesis of dissension, violence, intolerance, exclusivism and differences amongst different people, communities, cultures, religions, and so on. This will continue to plague our society unless and until each one of us realizes that no one subject or group can have or possess the totality of truth. Here comes the importance of looking at a reality from different angles apart from my own. In this regard, the ancient Jain texts explain two important concepts of *anekantvada* and *syadvada* with the parable of the *blind men and an elephant* (*Andhgajanyayah*), which addresses the manifold nature of truth. Let us see this parable:

A group of blind men heard that a strange animal called an elephant had been brought to the town but none of them were aware of its shape and form. Out of curiosity they said: "We must inspect and know it by touch, of which we are capable."

So, they sought it out and when they found it, they groped about it. In the case of the first person, whose hand landed on the trunk said, "This being is like a drain pipe". For another one whose hand reached its ear, it seemed like a kind of fan. As for another person, whose hand was upon its leg said, "I perceive the shape of the elephant to be like a pillar". And in the case of the one who placed his hand upon its back said, "Indeed, this elephant is like a throne". Now, each of these presented a true aspect when he related what he had gained from experiencing the elephant. None of them had strayed from the true description of the elephant. Yet, they fell short of fathoming the true appearance of the elephant. Each had partial truth about the elephant but not the whole.

Two of the many references to this parable are found in *Tattvarthaslokavatika* of *Vidyanandi* (9th century) and *Syadvadamanjari* of Acarya Mallisena (13th century). Mallisena uses the parable to argue that immature people deny various aspects of truth, deluded by the aspects they do understand, they deny the aspects they don't understand. Due to extreme delusion produced on account of a partial viewpoint, the immature denies one aspect and try to establish another. This is the maxim of the blind men and the elephant. Mallisena also cites the parable when noting the importance of considering all viewpoints in obtaining a full picture of reality. It is impossible to properly understand an entity consisting of infinite properties without the method of modal description consisting of all viewpoints, since it will otherwise lead to a situation of seizing mere sprouts (i.e., a superficial, inadequate cognition), on the maxim of the blind men and the elephant.

No one can comprehend the full truth of a reality. Therefore, I cannot claim to know the full truth of a reality. It would be wrong if one of the blind men says that elephant is only what he touched. This is not a wrong knowledge but only partial (incomplete truth). So, the partial cannot represent the whole. The truth is the whole. To reach the whole, all the viewpoints of the blind men have to be put together. The parable of the blind men and the elephant teaches us that to know something fully or the whole truth of any reality I need to accept the viewpoints of others.

Today, the chasm between different religions, cultures, ideologies, people and communities have become wider and wider because each one thinks that *"mine is the truth"*. Is not this subjectivism or collective subjectivism? This kind of mental positioning or paradigm will lead us to divide further and further and never allow us to meet and see each other's viewpoints. Instead of this, let us learn to view from each other's point, which will make the reality clear and gradually lead us to understand each other's view. Everyone possesses some truth. Let us take example of different religions. Hinduism is able to produce so many godly men like Swami Vivekananda, Rabindranath Tagore, Mahatma Gandhi and so on. Buddhism has also produced such holy men like Venerable Thich Nhat Hanh, His Holiness Dalai Lama and so on and Islam has also produced such holy men like Hazrat Shaik Abdul Jilani, and other Sufi saints and Christianity too has produced such godly persons like Mother Teresa, St. Francis of Assisi and Pope John Paul II, David Livingstone etc. The presence of all these good and holy people in these religions shows that there is goodness, and truth in all these religions. The goodness and truth of these religions is manifested in the holy persons they have produced. If all religions have possessed truth and goodness, we need to share with one another. This will enrich all of us. We need to relate in the spirit of "give and take". Sharing is a sign of love and oneness. Our life is meaningful only when we start sharing. God continues to share with us everything He has - air, water, food, sun, rain and so on. If God stops sharing just for a day what will happen to us? We know, we all will perish.

Let us therefore, not say, "Ours is the truth and others have to learn from us." Instead let us say, "Ours is good and other's also is good and therefore let us learn from them and let us also give the good that we have." This will create mutual benefit and love and peace will begin to operate among us. This will also destroy competition, comparison, pride, nonchalance, violence, and intolerance. John Locke has beautifully put it:

> *"We are all short-sighted and very often see but one side of a matter; our views are not extended to all that has a connection with it. From this defect I think no man is free. We see but in part, we know but in part and therefore, it is no wonder we conclude not right from our partial views. This might instruct the proudest esteemer of his own parts how useful it is to talk and consult with others, even such as come short of him in capacity, quickness and penetration; for since no one sees all and we generally have different prospect of the same thing according to our difference, as I may say positions to it, is not incongruous to think nor beneath any man to try, whether another man may not have notions of things which have escaped him and which his reason would make use of if they came into his mind."*

- *Learning and accepting the viewpoints of others will take you to a completely new and higher level of understanding and knowing the reality.*

61

Learn to Decide

"Be decisive, right or wrong, make a decision. The road of life is paved with flat squirrels who couldn't make a decision."

– Unknown

A person devoid of decisiveness will find his thoughts and dreams like vapours blown in the wind. He will go nowhere until he decides where should go. Life is made up of little decisions and big decisions and how a man decides determines the direction of his life. Decision is the spark that ignites action. Until a person makes a decision nothing happens. Decision is the difference maker. Why all my high school classmates today are doing different jobs? It's all because of their personal decisions. They decided to pursue their own interest areas and that is how they have landed up performing different careers. Our decisions have taken us all to different destinations in life. Decision can lead a person to the summit of a mountain. It can also make a person to fall to the valley below. But without decision nobody scales the mountain. It is better to risk a wrong decision rather than to make no decision at all.

Decision is not a blind chance. It is focusing the power of intelligence, meditation and prayer on the thing to be decided upon. Decision should not be made impetuously or randomly. Deciding to delay making a decision is a decision itself. If you want to be a good decision maker, you need to possess the following basic elements. They are as under:

(a) Be clear of your vision or goal in life.

(b) Be clear of your core values (the values/beliefs which you hold dear and for which you are ready to stand at all cost).

(c) Be impartial (take decision for the good of all).

(d) Be consultative (take opinions of experts/reliable people).

(e) Be analytical (weigh the possible consequences: merits and demerits)

If you have these fundamental elements, it will be a lot easier for you to take decisions in life. But if these elements are missing, you will find very tough to make decisions and even if you take decisions, the positivity of the result cannot be prognosticated. If the result turns out to be negative then it can cause further problem and sometimes one may not be able to control the consequence that come thereafter. It can sometimes cause more harm than good.

62

Lessons from King Asoka, the Great

"Good kings are slaves, and their people are free."

– Marie Leszczynska

King Asoka was one of the greatest emperors of all time. He was a Mauryan ruler whose kingdom spread across the Indian sub-continent and the present-day Pakistan and Afghanistan. He is known as Asoka, the Great, since, he was one of the most able rulers who ruled India. His life is an inspiration to many as he excelled in everything that he did. The name "Asoka" in Sanskrit means *"without any sorrow"*. He was crowned king of Magadha around 268 B.C. After a period of eight years of being a king, he planned to seize the territory of Kalinga, the present-day Orissa. He led a huge army and fought gruesome battle against the army of Kalinga. The battle took place on the banks of the river Daya.

The sight of numerous corpses lying strewn across the battlefield made his heart wrenched. He felt sick inside. The battleground looked like a graveyard with bodies of not just soldiers but men, women and children. Though Asoka emerged victorious at the end, the sight of the battlefield made his heart break with shame, guilt and disgust. It is said that the battle was so furious that the waters of River Daya turned red with the blood of the slain soldiers and civilians. This made him completely heartbroken and he made a pledge to never ever fight a battle again. To seek solace, he converted to Buddhism because he was so much inspired by the teachings of the Buddhist monks and philosophies. He became completely a changed person.

After the Kalinga war, he developed compassion for all human beings. His time table shows that he was a king who lived for the welfare of his people. He gave his time to his people. The following is his daily routine:

> *"The king gets up at 3 a.m. and till half past four examines various matters relating to the empire and takes decisions. He then receives the blessings of teachers and priests. Then he meets his doctors and the officials of the kitchen. He then goes to the court hall and considers from 6 a.m. to 7 a.m. the revenue and the expenditure of the previous day. From 7:30 he grants interviews to persons who have come to meet the emperor on urgent matters and examines their submissions. He retires to bathe at 9. After bath, prayer and breakfast, the emperor meets officers of the empire at 10:30 a.m. and issues instructions on many matters. All noon he meets the council of ministers and discusses matters of state. After rest between 1:30 to 3 p.m. he inspects the various divisions of the army. After this he receives reports from messengers and spies who have come from different parts of his empire and from other kingdoms."*

Asoka, who continued the ideal and the tradition of his grandfather Chandragupta, practiced in letter and spirit, the routine set down by Chanakya. Besides, Asoka believed that the prosperity of his subjects was his priority; so, he had appointed officers to report to him on the welfare and sufferings of the people. They were to report to him no matter what the hour was. His own order best shows his concern for the people. This is what he said: *"Whether I am dining or in my private apartments, asleep or engaged in some work, setting out on a journey or resting; wherever I may be and whatever the time of the day or night the officers must come and report to me about the people and their affairs. Wherever I maybe I shall think about the welfare of the people and work for them.*"

A beautiful administrative advice:

After Asoka defeated Kalinga, he then appointed officers to administer the kingdom. How do officers who go from the victorious state to the defeated land usually behave towards the people? They lose all sense of justice and fair play and behave proudly. They insult the defeated people. Asoka did not want this to happen. He desired that the people of Kalinga should live in peace and honour. This was his order to the officers who were sent to Kalinga:

> "*I have put you in charge of thousands of people. Earn the love and affection of all those people. Whatever situation may arise treat all people alike. Be impartial in your actions. Give up rudeness, haste, laziness and lack of interest and short temper. Nothing can be achieved if we are bored and idle. Therefore, be active. If you understand how sacred your work is and behave with a sense of responsibility, you will go to heaven and you will also repay your debt to the king who appointed you.*" Asoka who treated his subjects as his children further said, "*Like a mother who gives her child to an able nurse, trusting that she would bring up the baby well. I have entrusted my subjects to your care.*"

63

Levels of Relationship

"I love my eyes when you look into them. I love my name when you say it. I love my heart when you touch it. I love my life when you are in it."
– Unknown

Relationship can be of different levels. All relationships are not the same. Relationship can be established in varying degrees. It can be intense, less intense or just normal or casual. It can also be intensely selfish, intensely selfless and it can be just normal (neither intensely selfish not intensely selfless). It can be divided into three levels. They are put as under:

Level - 1 Relationship (L1R): The first level relationship is based on the principle *'Pahale Main"*. *Pahale Main* is a Hindi phrase which means *"Me First"*. This is intensely selfish relationship. So, the priority of this relationship is the fulfilling of "My Needs" first. If a relationship does not satisfy 'my needs', it is not worth remaining in that relationship. Here, one is aware of only one's own needs and completely oblivious of the other person's needs. This is the immature level. This is a relationship which is most unhealthy to enter in. If one enters into relationship with such selfish person, one should be willing to give up all his or her needs in order to serve the needs of that person. Otherwise, the relationship is not going to work out. It is egoistic pursuit at its peak. Selfishness has no limits and therefore, even if one is willing to sacrifice all his/her needs, the egoistic person will never be satisfied. Relationship usually don't work out at this level.

Level - 2 Relationship (L2R): At this level, relationship functions on the principle of *quid pro quo* (a favour for a favour). It is a Latin phrase which literally means *"something for something"*. *You give mine and You take yours* or *You get yours and I get mine*. Here, relationship is a contract of favours. Records are maintained for the number of favours done to the other. The danger of this relationship is that when there is imbalance in the favour tally, tension increases and in course of time if this imbalance is not rectified, it can cause a serious problem. Here, each one is counting the favours done to the other. It is a very complicated relationship where the favour done must be reciprocated on time; otherwise, delaying can be a source of tension. It is a mutual reciprocation of each other's needs on time. It is conditional relationship. When relationship is conditional; it is very difficult to sustain.

Level - 3 Relationship (L3R): At this level, relationship is founded on the principle of "*App Pahale*". *Aap Pahale* is a Hindi phrase which means "You First". Here, a person joyfully puts the other person's needs first and ready let go his or her needs in order to make the other person happy. This is the strongest relationship based on VALUES (love, forgiveness, humility, compassion, empathy etc.). Relationship here has no record of favours, no conditions, and expects nothing in return. Above all, it enjoys giving and serving the other person. This relationship provides people with a sense of identity and belonging.

Among the levels, the third level is the best level in relationship. It takes hard work and continuous effort to build this Level 3 Relationship. In order to build L3R, one requires certain relationship skills. They are as stated as under:

1. *Affective Understanding:* This means you understand people with your heart and not with your mind. Feelings come from the heart. So, feel, what they feel and you will know their heart beats. After feeling their heart beats, you can dance according to the beats and you will

see that relationship is a celebration. If you don't cultivate affective understanding, relationship can sink into indifference. When that happens, even birth day celebration can turn into black day celebration.

2. *Clarity of Communication:* Clarity of communication means whatever and whenever you communicate, it must be clear and easily understood. Your communication must be smooth, soothing and enhancing and not hurting or harmful. Most of the broken relationships began with "communication gap" (retirement from talking to the other person). Do not give chance for this 'gap' to come into your relationship.
3. *Recognize and Compliment People:* If you practice, recognizing the good people do and give them positive strokes like 'Well-done!', 'Congratulations!', 'Nice of you!', 'You are so sweet!', 'You are so thoughtful!', you will indeed win their hearts. Do not be afraid to recognize and compliment people. By practicing this, people will recognize and compliment you more.
4. *Practice Accountability:* Accountability here, means owning up one's mistakes. In a relationship, whenever I hurt the other, I am ready to say "Sorry" than throw the blame on the other. Since, I value the relationship, I am ready to 'wrong' myself even if I may be right. I will not justify over my mistakes and allow my ego to go out of control. I am ready to bend myself in order to make the other person happy.
5. *Avoid Nit-picking:* Nit-picking can be a deadly virus infecting relationship. Nit-picking is the habit of finding small mistakes in somebody's work or paying too much attention to small, unimportant details. Why to pay attention to small and unimportant details when it is not important. Just turn a blind eye over these unimportant details. Pay attention only to important and essential ones. If nit-picking enters into relationship,

it will gradually destroy the peace and calm in a relationship which can further cause havoc if it becomes chronic. A nitpicky person is incapable of sustaining relationship.

6. *Avoid Suspicion:* Suspicion is one of the most dangerous pathogens that incapacitates relationship. Suspicion destroys 'trust' which is the very foundation of every relationship. Once, suspicion enters relationship and is allow to grow, it can be predicted that such relationship is on the way to its destruction. Suspicion is believing rumours as fact. It has no proofs and evidence. It is a foundationless information. Therefore, without verifying facts, never, ever believe in rumours. Believing rumours can be harmful to relationship.
7. *Accept and Celebrate Differences:* Relationship ultimately is about accepting the other person as he or she is, without expecting anything in return. I can't change a person who has a different genetic code and brought up in different setting or environment for years. I can't expect such person to adapt to my ways. It will be painful for a person to fit into another person's system. Therefore, the best is to learn from each other and adapt to each other's system. Whatever can be adapted, adapt them and whatever can't be adapted accept them happily. Acceptance is the password to happiness and expectation is the password to frustration. Real love is accepting those elements which are different from mine in the other person. Whatever I do, I do out of love, expecting nothing in return.

64

Life Is to Be Shared

"He who does not live in some degree for others hardly lives for himself."
– Montaigne

Life is given to me and this is given to me because of the largesse of the Creator. If He has given and shared His life with me then, I also in turn need to give and share my life with others. Life is not given exclusively for me alone. I am given so that I may SHARE. Life is a gift and it is a holy gift for its Giver is holy. Life is an extension of His life. Because of this, life is sacred, beautiful and good. Realizing this sacredness, LIFE must be loved, cared and shared. So, if life is so sacred, so beautiful and so good, we must do the following homework daily:

I must love my life
I must care my life
I must share my life

You must love your life
You must care your life
You must share your life

We must love our lives
We must care our lives
We must share our lives

Will it not be beautiful if we do this homework every day of our life?

Every individual is unique, special and unrepeatable. He has a role to play and contribute to the totality of humanity's good and if a person fails to do this, then, the whole humanity will suffer the loss. Every individual has the sacred duty to contribute something to the progress and development of the whole human community. It is of paramount importance to be other-oriented than self-oriented. What I do for the humanity is as important as what I do for myself. Sometimes, how nice it is to hear from somebody that "this person is always helping others that he does not have time for himself." Let us ruminate the words of Baden Powel, the founder of the Boys Scout Movement, *"Try and leave this world a little better than you found it..."*

Do not pass by this world without contributing a mite to humanity. The humanity should not suffer the loss caused by your miserliness. Many have passed by this world in silence without contributing anything. They have forgotten that it is their duty to better this world.

65

Life is To Be Celebrated

"Life is what you celebrate. All of it. Even its end."

– Joanne Harris

John Powell in his book "*The Secret of Staying in Love*" writes, "I am convinced that man was meant to live at peace within himself with deep joy. I am convinced that there should be going on in the heart of every man not a funeral but a celebration of life and love. Prophets of gloom, with their valley of tears mentality and vocabulary, have always believed that 'the glory of God is a man fully alive!' Of course! there is no problem- less Camlot or painless Utopia. The tension resulting from problems and pain is part of the whole piece and usually directs our attention to a growing edge of life, a territory for expansion. For myself, I do not regret the problems or pain in my past life, but only the apathy, the moments when I was not fully alive".

Life must be celebrated and not turn into a funeral cortege. A fully-alive-person is a celebration of life itself and life must be celebrated every moment of our life. Celebration of life does not mean '*an all-time merriment*'. This kind of celebration is impossible for most part of our life is made up of unhappiness and sufferings of all sorts as Thomas Hardy puts it, *"Happiness is but an occasional episode in the general drama of life"*. So, '*Celebration of life*' means *a joyful acceptance of all that is pleasant and unpleasant in life*. The problems of life should not deplete all our attention and energy. Moments of problems should be converted into episodes of celebration.

- *An uncelebrated life is a life not alive.*

66

Life is Brief!

"I guess the real fact of the matter is, we don't know what tomorrow is going to bring and the only thing we really have is right now. So, don't stay mad for too long. Learn to forgive. Love with all your heart. Have fun. Live your life the way you want to live it. Don't worry about people that don't like. Enjoy the ones who do."

- Unknown

The shortness of our life must sooner drive us to live our life more meaningfully than just merely exist. To live meaningfully, our life must be filled with benevolence as Amiel exhorts us, *"Life is short and we have never too much time for gladdening the hearts of those who are travelling the dark way with us. Oh, be swift to love! Make haste to be kind"*. Henry Burton has given us a practical and meaningful way of living our life thus:

Have you had a kindness shown?
Pass it on
'Twas not given for thee alone,
Pass it on
Let it travel down the years,
Let it wipe another's tears,
Till in heaven the deed appears-
Pass it on
Did you hear the loving word?
Pass it on

Like the singing of a bird?
Pass it on
Let its music live and grow
Let it cheer another's woe,
You have reaped what
others sow-
Pass it on.
Twas the sunshine of a
Smile -
Pass it on
April beams a little thing.
Still, it wakes the flowers of
Spring,
Makes the silent birds sing
Pass it on".

Do not break the chain of passing on? We are given to give and not to hoard.

67

Life is a Challenge, Fight It Out

"Strive and thrive!" cry, "Speed – fight on, fare ever...!"

– Robert Browning in 'Asolando'

There is no battle fiercer than the battle that is fought within oneself. It is so fierce because this battle has to be fought in the moral space. The battle *without* is easy for there are myriads of lethal weapons which you can take recourse to. Anyone who has an AK-47 rifle will say that he has no fear of his enemy. Contrariwise, one cannot resort to such lethal weapons in the battle *within*. In the battle *within*, the enemy is more shrewd, wily and subtle than the enemy in the battle *without*. The enemy is that which prevents us from doing good and to fight this out one needs to have a strong inbuilt system or a strong moral stamina. The moral stamina includes:

- The courage to stand for one's principles.
- The courage to stand against what is evil (selfishness, hatred, envy, jealousy, violence, corruption etc).
- The courage to endure daily sufferings like boredom, anxiety, stress, tension, and frustration of life.

The battle within is beautifully expressed in the song "*Jekyll and Hyde*" by the all-time-great Gospel rock band *Petra*. The lyrics run thus:

I have a secret that I let nobody see

An evil shadow that's been hanging over me

My alter ego that I try to hold at bay
But despite my good intentions he could always get away
He does the things that I don't want to do

Sometimes I feel like Jekyll and Hyde
Two men are fighting a war inside

I have a secret that I let nobody see
It's like a split personality
And the one I feed is the one who lives
The one I starve will be the one who gives
He won't do things that I know I should do

Sometimes I feel like Jekyll and Hyde
Two Men are fighting a war inside
One gives, one takes, I have to decide
Sometimes I feel like... Jekyll and Hyde

I need somebody to rescue me
when personalities clash
I know which person I want to be
With no defiance, just God-reliance

- *Are you ready to fight?*

68

Life Must Be Played

"Life is like the Olympic games; a few men strain their muscles to carry off a prize, others sell trinkets to the crowd for a profit; some just came to look and see how everything is done." – **Pythagoras**

The world in which we live and move is like a mighty stadium. In this stadium, there are three kinds of people performing different roles. They are:

- The players
- The spectators
- The chatters

The first group of people comes to the Stadium to PLAY and to WIN. They come with the singular aim of winning. Nothing can distract them. They work very hard to prepare themselves in order to play and win. They constantly strive till their goal is achieved. They are ever active, enthusiastic, effervescent, cheerful and ready to face any challenge in the competition. They are the cynosure in the stadium.

The second group of people comes to the stadium not to play but to SEE. They see and enjoy the game of the players from a distance. The aim of these people is just to see and not to play. In real life if you ask this type of people, to perform any task, their answer will be nothing but "let me see". For anything and everything, their answer remains the same. They are viewers of life and have only time for seeing and not playing. They fear action and prefer to live in an utopian paradise.

The third group of people comes to the stadium just to barter their time in pastime. They come to the stadium to socialize. They chat with one another and squander their precious time. They take delight in current events, high sounding philosophies and so on. They are neither interested in the players nor seeing them. They are interested in their own petty affairs and take delight in blarney. These people neither understand life nor value life. They are contented with peripheral existence. They passed this beautiful stadium without leaving a footprint on it.

Life is not to be seen from a distance or to be squandered. It must be played and won. Otherwise it is only a futile existence.

- *To which of the three categories do you belong?*

69

Life Is Worth Living

"A man who dares to waste one hour of time has not discovered the value of life." – **Charles Darwin**

Life is the greatest gift that is given to human beings. It is supremely good and beautiful. Therefore, it is the most valuable and precious gift from God. There is a *Yoruba* (ethnic group that inhabits western Africa) word that describes the sublimity of life. That word is, "*Agreyewoanu*" which means *"Life does everything"*. In other words, it means with life we can do all things. Life is a wonderful gift with which we can do almost everything.

Life becomes useful and meaningful only if it is understood. Thus, the old wise philosopher Socrates said, "*The unreflected life isn't worth living*". To understand one's life, one must reflect and meditate. Once you reflect, you will understand and once you understand you will know the purpose and once you know the purpose, you have discovered what life is. Here is pertinent, the words of Venerable Thich Nhat Hanh, a Vietnamese monk who was nominated for the Nobel Peace Prize by Martin Luther King Jr. in 1967. He said, "*Meditation's purpose is to be aware of what is going on in ourselves and in the world. What is going on in the world can be seen within ourselves and vice versa. Once you see this clearly you cannot refuse to take position but act*".

- *Understanding of one's thoughts, feelings and actions is a conditio sine qua non for worthwhile living.*

70

Listen to The Cry of a Girl

"A man doesn't need to be flawless to be a perfect father, but the commitment to his family is a precious responsibility."

– Paul Young

I am an eight year old girl. My name is Betsy. Since my family is very poor, my parents have no means to send me to school. My father is a dipsomaniac and comes home late everyday getting drunk and used to beat my mother. I play with my friends during the day and when evening comes, we stop our games and leave for our homes. All my friends used to go home with great joy and happiness. For them, home is a place of joy and love, their parents welcome them with an embrace and kisses of love. Once they reach home they are on the laps of their mothers. But as for me when evening comes, I begin to feel afraid and insecure. I know that unlike my friends, I will not be welcomed at home. So, I don't want evening to come, I want day to be long. I wish that the sun never sets. As I draw near my home my fear increases and with tremor, I approach my house. When I enter my home, no one is there to welcome me; no attention is given to me. I can only see my father in a drunken stupor beating up my innocent mother who works so hard for the family the whole day. Nobody knows the pain I am going through. Sometimes, I used to curse myself why I was born. I wish if I were never born. Sometimes, I think of ending my life but a second thought used to tell me that there is God who can do everything. He can change and transform people. With this glimpse of hope simmering in my heart, I go on in my life and say a small prayer for my Dad every day.

This is the general drama taking place in every family where the father of the family is an alcoholic. The family members suffer terribly but they are helpless. How will children grow in such atmosphere? When the family is beset by violence, hate, and fights; it is most unhealthy for children to grow. A doctor once asked a young girl, "What does home mean to you?" she replied, "Home is a place you go when it gets dark." A child who can return to the security of a loving home when it gets dark is blessed indeed. How sad that for many children today home is all darkness.

- *O, family man! Remember each time you get drunk; you are causing pain in your lovely child. If you want her to grow, stop drinking. Your child needs no beating but love and attention. Give love and attention and in someday you will see your child blooming.*

71

Living in the Irrational World

"Man stands face to face with the irrational. He feels within him his longing for happiness and for reason. The absurd is born of this confrontation between the human need and the unreasonable silence of the world." **– Albert Camus, The Myth of**

Sisyphus and Other Essays The world is at times very irrational, inhuman, nonchalant and utterly silent when we want a response. In this murky and cloudy world, we are seeking for clarity but no clarity seems to come from anywhere. This is the absurdity of life. Things get worsened and existence becomes unbearable at times. What can be the solution many say? Some come to the conclusion that existence is meaningless and hopeless and so the best solution is escape from this life by introducing themselves to drugs or commit suicide. But to do this would be a passive resignation to the absurdities of life. To succumb to these absurdities would amount to an act of cowardice.

The way to counter the absurdities is to follow the way of revolution. Life will become meaningful only when we live in what Albert Camus says as *a proud conscious revolt against the absurdities of life*. We must fight against the absurdities of our existence. The absurdities of life are irrationality, inhumanity, indifference, silence, loneliness and so on. When you really need the help of somebody, you just get the exact opposite. You experience what is known as *"situational irony"* - you expect one thing and the exact opposite happens. You expect your best friend to visit you when you are laying on your sick bed but he doesn't even pick your call. He knows but he doesn't even care to say 'Hello!'. When you deserve appreciation, you just get criticism. When you need sympathy, you just get alienation. When you want a solution to your life's problems, what you get is only silence. Nobody wants to stand by you and vindicate you. We see that the good people are struggling and the bad people seem to be thriving. Is not this irrational and ironic? I don't know when we are going to usher into the land of rationality and clarity. Let us not give up in life. Let us be a bit rebellious i.e., being courageous and accountable in our lives. Let us keep fighting, even if we see a slim chance of victory in the battle. It is not important to win the battle but it is also noble to die in the fight. Che Guevara says, *"Better to die standing than to live on your knees."*

- *I am not a coward but revolutionary.*

72

Look at No One as Your Enemy (for Civil Leaders)

"Everybody you fight is not your enemy and everybody that helps you is not your friend." – **Mike Tyson**

Mahatma Gandhi was a devotee of truth and non-violence. Once a man who was a student leader during the freedom struggle of India tells of an interview he had with Mahatma Gandhi. He visited him to ask for his blessing on a strike they had intended to organize. *"When I explained the purpose of my visit, he said an interesting thing. 'Yes, I am interested that you want to go on strike but number one, be sure that the cause for which you are going on strike is based on nothing but pure and absolute truth.' The second thing he said was, 'Be sure if you go on this strike that you have no hatred of the Englishman, that you have no hate or bitterness towards anyone in your heart.' And the third thing he said was, 'Love the police and those who will be your enemies on the other side.' Then he said, 'If you are absolutely convinced about the truth of your cause, then you can also be sure that God and His strength will be behind you.'"*

There are some valuable lessons one can learn from the advice given by Gandhiji to the student leader. This is very relevant in our times too when there are a lot of strikes and protests used as a means to achieve one's end. Let us analyze some of the things Gandhi has spoken.

(i) ***"be sure... pure and absolute truth":*** Any civil leader, who wants to achieve their goals from the government through strike or protest must make sure first that the cause he is going to take up is based on pure and absolute truth. The opposite of "Truth" is 'lie', 'falsehood', 'deceit', 'deception', 'dishonesty', 'selfish motive', 'duplicity' and 'fraud'. The leader must be absolutely clear of the purpose for which he is going for a strike or protest. He must be clear of what he is doing and why he is doing? The cause that the leader undertakes must be free from lie, deceit, deception, dishonesty, selfish motive, duplicity and fraud. It should not be based on any selfish motive and personal benefits. The leaders must be free from all deceits and falsehood. Those who follow the leader, repose their trust in him because they know that he is reliable, honest and sincere for them. In course of time, if the followers come to know his selfish motive and personal gains, that person will lose his credibility and finally he will be left alone without followers.

(ii) ***"have no hate or bitterness towards anyone in your heart":*** After clarifying the motive of the movement, the next is to make sure that the cause is launched not out of hatred but for justice and truth. Therefore, no hatred must be allowed to take control of those fighting for the cause. If it is based on hatred, it will instantly turn into violence and violence can lead to bloodshed and if it results in bloodshed, the matter will get complicated and finally it will be difficult to resolve the problem. Every leader also must realize that life is the highest value and it must be protected at all cause. It will be meaningless to fight for freedom and after the fight there is no one to enjoy that freedom. It will be like what the Bible says, "What does it profit a man if he conquers the whole world but loses his life?" Therefore, the leaders must ensure that life is valued and respected and must be protected from all harms even during strikes and protests.

(iii) ***'Love the police and those who will be your enemies on the other side":*** When the strike is launched first whom you are going to face is the police. Gandhi says that the strikers must love the police and those who will be your enemies on the other side. Many may say that this is absolutely utopian - to love the enemies and get what you want from them. But Gandhi is speaking from his experience. Since, love works, he is suggesting it. Therefore, the purpose of the cause is to get justice and truth and not to destroy the people who are to dispense what is being fought for.

The weapons that Mahatma Gandhi used were truth and non-violence. He himself proved that these weapons were powerful. Subash Chandra Bose didn't believe in soft weapons like truth and non-violence. When the enemy is so unjust, violent, and untruthful, how can you trust and fight with love? Yet, Subash Chandra Bose too, had his own way of looking at the independence movement. Though many may view Gandhi critically; yet, the fact that his own enemies speak about him shows that he is an extraordinary personality. Lord Mountbatten, the last Viceroy of India said, *"India indeed, the world will not see the like of him again."* When he died in 1948, Albert Einstein said, *"Generations to come will scarce that such a one as this ever in flesh and blood walked upon this earth."* Dr. Ishwari Prasad, a notable historian said, "*The death of Mahatma Gandhi marks the close of an epoch in Indian history. It was an epoch of great events, when by means of truth and non-violence without any battalions or armies, this frail little man shook the mightiest empire to its foundations.*" In 1959 Martin Luther King made a trip to Gandhi's country, who is his source of inspiration and said, "*To other countries I may go as a tourist. But to India I come as a pilgrim.*" Indians refers to him as *"American Gandhi."* Martin Luther King also said, *"From my background, I gain my regulating Christian ideals. From Gandhi, I learned my operational technique".* Louis Fischer, a reputed American journalist said, *"I have met Lenin, Churchill, Franklin D. Roosevelt, Wilkie, Stalin, Litvinov, Attlee, Einstein, Lloyd George, Eleanor Roosevelt and many other famous people. I have never met a more remarkable person than Gandhi".*

73

Love

"My love for you is not a gift to you but it is a gift to me."

– Leonard Nimoy

Love is the meeting point of "God and man" and "man and man". It is the supreme principle through which deeper to deepest relationships are established. Philosophically, we can define love as the supreme quality by which the finite touches the Infinite and his fellow finite beings. It is the philosophic principle, which harmonizes and unifies all beings. It is the creative cause, sustaining and perfecting power. A life devoted to love is ennobling indeed and leads man higher and higher. The real worth of a person is known by the amount of love he can generate. A life lived without love is not worth living.

Love loves and loves everything

A person who loves Love, is Love and loves everything

A person, who loves Love, loves a person

A person, who loves a person, loves that person's *entirety* (all that a person is). Therefore,

- **To love** a person means to love him *as he or she is* and not as *he or she is not.*
- **To love means *to liberate*** i.e., seeking the autonomous growth of the other person. I want the person to grow

as he or she should grow and not as I am or I want him or her to be. I don't determine or direct him/her. This is called liberating love.

- To love also means *to decide* i.e. Love is a decision and therefore, I decide to love a person whether he or she deserves my love or not. I decide to love a person who is not worthy of love. Once decided, I don't give up on him/her. I am committed to my decision and no alteration whatsoever.
- To love also means to see and recognize a person as a *meta-being* i.e. a person originating from the *meta-world* or God. A person is a *meta-reality.* I love everything that comes from God as sacred and holy. In loving a person, I am proving my love for God.

> *"Love is not simply giving; it is judicious giving and judicious withholding as well. It is judicious praising and judicious criticizing. The word 'judicious' means requiring judgment and judgment requires more than instinct; it requires thoughtful and often painful decision-making".*
>
> – M. Scott Peck in *The Road Less Travelled*

74

Man is a Reflective or Rational Being

"Passions lay man below the beasts, whereas mind makes him equal to immortal." – **Petar Petrovic Njegos, a Yugoslav poet**

A certain philosopher defined MAN as "*Thought thinking thought*". In other words, man is a meta-cognitive being. Man is a thought which thinks a thought. This is because he is endowed with the faculty of thinking and that differentiates and elevates him from all other beings. He is the most complex of all beings. One of the basic differences between a human being and other beings is that '*other beings are not capable of becoming a human being. But human beings are capable of becoming an animal through degeneration or reverse evolution of his rational and moral instinct*'. Repetitive evolution or re-evolution cannot change an animal into human beings. This is impossible because there is an unalterable set-pattern of the law of nature. The law of nature does not permit animals to evolve into human beings. Man was created with a great design and he is the peak of creation. Though he is a sublime being, he is capable of becoming a declined being. He can evolve into sub-human form through moral degeneration. He is also capable of transforming himself from human being to being human (which is higher than being a mere human being). The transition from human-ness to animalism can take place when man stops using his faculty of reason and ethicality.

When can man stop reasoning and being reasonable? When he is completely controlled by his emotion i.e., when he is under the regime of his emotion. This can cause a hitch in his rational existence. An uncontrolled or unguided emotion can be potentially and fatally dangerous. Therefore, the wild animal in us must be tamed. One of the analogies between man and animal is that both have instincts. But, while man can tame his instincts, animals cannot. Man can do this by using his reason. Through the power of reason, he can conquer his irrationalities. For example, man in his extreme hunger can still think and then decide not to take food or delay. But animal is not capable of that. Here, we see that reasoning is followed by decision. Reasoning and decision are two vital qualities that qualify and make human beings so different from animals. But if you subtract these two qualities, you will find that man is not man but MAD and is worse than animal. All great inventions and discoveries and achievements are the upshot of deep reflection. Due to this, it is of gargantuan importance that one reflects before he takes any step.

O, Man! Know that you are the most superior of all beings. You are an intelligent animal but animal is not an intelligent man. I am nonplus at your abysmal intelligence and dexterity. I would never agree with Bertrand Russel who said that you are "*...the outcome of accidental collocations of atoms....*" Any reflective being would not subscribe to this statement for there is a great design and intelligence involved behind your being. Blaise Pascal once said, "*Man is greater than the world for the world does not know when it is falling, but man knows when the world is falling on him.*"

75

Man, The Unsolved Miracle

O, MAN! You are the most miraculous miracle,
All that is in you is a miracle,
You are a miracle.
There is an unfathomable power within you,
There is still a lot of untapped potential,
Your heart and mind are springs of miracle,
O, miracle man.

O, MAN! You are a contradictory miracle,
You turn happiness into sadness,
You turn love into hate,
You turn friends into foe,
You turn saints into sinners,
You turn peace into war.

There is a negative power operating within you,
Your heart and mind are springs of chaos,
You are so disorderly,
You are a contradictory miracle,
You are an unsolved miracle.

– Stephen Touthang

76

M Goi Nei

Archbishop Fulton J. Sheen in his autobiography *"Treasure in Clay"* writes the story of an American missionary nun who worked in China. When she returned back home from China, she related the following experience thus: Each day as the Communist soldiers would allow prisoners to walk in the prison yard for exercise, they would do two things: first, barely open the prison gate so that they had to squeeze through it with great pain and exertion; second, they would spit in the face of each missionary that passed. One day after a soldier spat in her face, the sister said, *"M goi nei,"* which in Chinese means "Thank You!"

- *Learn to say "Thank You!" even when it is tough.*

77

Martin Heidegger: A Human Person and His Situation

> *"Anyone can achieve their fullest potential, who we are might be predetermined, but the path we follow is always of our own choosing. We should never allow our fears or expectations of others to set the frontiers of our destiny. Your destiny can't be changed but, it can be challenged."*
> **- Martin Heidegger**

Martin Heidegger, a German philosopher and seminal thinker was an ex-Jesuit novice who continued to pursue his philosophical studies and went beyond the fame of Sartre. He was a hardcore existentialist who stresses the aspects of human aesthetic and passionate nature – freedom, guilt, anguish, love and so on. Martin Heidegger analyses an individual human being in relation to himself, his environment and to other human beings. He says that the individual's existence is temporary and finite. So, finitude becomes the cause of anguish in him. Together with finitude the individual realizes that there is an end (death). So, he concludes that a human being is *"a being unto death."* This inevitability of death is causing meaningless vacuum in the life of human beings.

According to Heidegger the human existence displays three fundamental aspects:

(a) *Factuality:* This refers to the human rootedness in the past. Every person has their own history. I am nothing but the by-product or epiphenomenon of history. All my thoughts and actions are conditioned by my history. It is this historicity that is affecting my present existence. So, the past contributes a gigantic portion of my present (being -ness). So, he speaks about "*Thrownness*" (Geworfenheit) which means that a human person is thrown into this complex existence (past and present mixed up), which I did not choose. I did not choose my life, my family, my culture, and my history. I am *being thrown* (geworfen) in a situation where I do not want to be. This situation in German is called *"Dasein"* (German: *da* "there", *sien* "being"). It literally means *"being there"*. The ultimate error is that I was not consulted for anything that happens in my past.

(b) *Existentiality:* Human existentiality is hard to accept or compromise. But in such a hard-existential situation, a human person is capable of courageous resolute or decisive action. He can courageously assimilate his past (accept it) and accept responsibility for the present. This is an authentic freedom. He must re-define himself. According to Heidegger, a cat doesn't concern itself with being a cat, a tree doesn't concern itself with being a tree, but a person does concern himself with being certain kind of person (a builder, painter, woman, parent and so on). This is because, unlike cats or trees, he defines his own being as he goes along. He is continually faced with challenges and possibilities from among which he can choose and through his choices, he overcomes the challenges and actualizes or redefines himself. Heidegger also says that a person has to carry out his choices courageously. Therefore, living the life of a person is a matter of constantly

(i) Taking a stand on who we are.

(ii) Being defined as who we are by taking that stand (no choice is 'once and for always' so we have to keep on choosing to be who we are).

(iii) Added to these, the being of everything else on the planet is also an issue for us because we deal with things as what they are and persons as who they are. So, we relate with human beings as meaningfulness is realized. The term Heidegger uses for this is *Mitsein* which means a human being is a being with others.

(c) *Fallenness:* Human beings today are submerged in the world situation. The world situation that humans created today is a world of tools and opportunities. We have become manufacturers, consumers and collectors of tools and gadgets. This is how the common man (crowd/general) functions. When a person follows the ways of the crowd or general, he becomes the *Das Man* (the average depersonalised individual who thinks feels and acts like the general public). *Das Man* literally means "*they-self*". Every individual is supposed to work and attain their "*authentic self*" (my owned self) but many have turned into "*the they-self*" (my un-owned self). The majority of the human beings have metamorphosed into the *Das Man*. This is the *fallenness* of human beings. Due to the world situation, human beings are not able to relate with other human beings meaningfully. But Heidegger says that a human being is a being with others. In German it is called *Mitsein* (Being-with). Human beings find their true meaning in being with others i.e., by relatedness. According to Heidegger, we live in a world shared with others (shared meanings and shared situation). There is a shared, public nature of the self. *Mitsein*, then is about the ways in which we write ourselves on to others and others write themselves onto us. Because our world is made up of others who use the same language and tools as we use, and we cannot define ourselves or our world without reference to others. Being-alone then becomes a way of being-with because you need to be in the same world with others in order to even conceive a concept like "being-alone". Therefore, human beings are ultra-social and obligatorily gregarious.

A few takeaways from Hiedegger's ideas on a human existence:

1. Human existence is finite and therefore, there is a need to expedite our search for meaning in life.
2. The factuality of human beings is that they are *thrown* into this complex world. We should not despair because our existence is characterized by *Geworfenheit* (Thrownness). This means that we were not given a choice with regards to our individual's life, family, culture, history etc. We were just *being thrown* (geworfen) into a situation where each of us do not want to be. But despairing over our present existence (past + present) is not going to benefit or solve our problems. So, the best is, let us accept the facticity (existential realities consisting of difficulties and struggles of life) of our situation and re-define ourselves and find meaning in life.
3. We re-define our lives by making informed choices. Our choices will make us usher into a new self. The choices we make today will transform who we will be tomorrow. If one makes good choices, he will become good person tomorrow. If one makes great choices today, he will become great tomorrow. If one makes a hopeless choice, he will become hopeless tomorrow. We become what we choose. Our choices will define us, who we are!
4. Once we make a firm and resolute decision/s, we must be committed and take responsibility for those decisions that we have made.
5. We must not be complacent with our *fallenness* but rise above it. We must overcome the *Das Man* (average man) and go beyond by becoming *Mitsein* (being capable of meaningful relationship).

78

Mother Earth

"Earth provides enough to satisfy every man's NEED but not every man's GREED."
- Gandhi

An American journalist once asked Osho, "How important do you think the use of the land is, in general, in terms of the development of human spirituality or society?" The following is his answer: "It has tremendous importance. It is our mother, the earth. We may not see them but we also have roots in the earth. We are walking trees. The earth supplies everything to us. I am against a god who is far away in the heaven but I am not against the mother earth. We should make it enriched; we should not disturb the balance of nature, which we have been doing for centuries. I am absolutely in favour of nature, its balance. We should not do anything that goes against it because finally that goes against us. We are part of this earth. So, land should be used respectfully, lovingly. Working with the earth – farming, gardening – you are doing real religious work, enriching the earth and helping the earth to regain its lost resources. I am absolutely in favour of those environmentalists who want to save the environment against the rape that man has done with his own mother. The earth has been raped badly everywhere and something has to be done urgently because the earth is dying".

The need of the hour is that human beings need to renew and pledge once again their love for the Mother Earth. We call

'Mother Earth' because she has been providing us everything that we need - for our survival and comfort. As Osho said, we have abused our mother so much that she is dying. Which human being will allow his mother to die? Mother Earth is the mother of all mothers. She has been feeding and providing all the needs of human beings from the beginning of human existence without any complain. This is the right moment, to come together take a stand that our common Mother should no longer be abused. We must show all gratitude for feeding and providing so many countless generations and now it is high time for us to show our love and respect for her and know that without her we can't survive.

79

Mutual Respect

Deem every person as a mine rich in gems of immeasurable value.

Erik Blumenthal in his book, "*Understand and Be Understood*" writes, "*Mutual respect is one of the most important rules for a good relationship. Without this respect, there can be no real equality between individuals or within groups of people. Without a deep understanding of equality and mutual respect, there cannot be peace.*"

Respect for a person springs from deep understanding. Understanding can be of two types: *sympathetic* and *antipathetic* understanding. In *antipathetic understanding*, one is advertently oblivious of the other person's goodness or positivity. This is a negative understanding of a person. Here, one tries to understand only the negative side of the other person. In other words, the person is antipathetic towards the other person. In *sympathetic understanding*, one is advertently sympathetic towards the other person. Here, one understands the other person's capabilities and weaknesses. Understanding here means not merely knowing a person, it means the obverse reading of the word UNDERSTANDING i.e., STANDING-UNDER OTHERS:

UNDER-STANDING
Means → OTHERS
STANDING-UNDER

"Standing-Under-Others" means humbling oneself before others. Humbling oneself before others does not mean that the other person is so great and I am only a nonentity or a small fry. No! It means acceptance of the other person with sympathetic humility. I know that I am also good enough though it may not be in the same field of talents as the other person is. Here, humbling oneself means I choose to adopt "standing- under-others" as a sympathetic attitude towards others because I value relationship.

In order to live in mutual respect, one should not adopt names like smart alec, braggart, poseur or swaggerer etc. because such appellations are pompous classification of oneself from others. The attitude of a smug person is potentially dangerous for it can instantly jeopardize respect for others. Under such attitude, mutual respect is impossibility. Such person will never come to the rank of others.

Mutual respect is not unilateral but bilateral. To cultivate mutual respect, I must first frame my attitude. It should be a well-balanced attitude of an equalization of oneself with the rank of the other. This is an attitudinal equalization. There should be mutual initiative for mutual respect. Only this *mutual initiative* is the beginning of mutual respect. One should not deem oneself as lower or higher than the other. There should be a feeling of *equal-ness* with the other person. This is not pride but confidence. One should neither feel lower nor higher than the other person. This is treating the other person as well as myself with dignity and respect.

80

My Heart Works 24 Hours to Make Me Live

"What is stronger than the human heart which shatters over and over and still lives." – **Rupi Kaur**

Throughout the parts of human body, there is a network of tubes, which in an average adult extend a total distance of 10,000 miles. They make up the circulatory system - combination of water main, central heating, main drainage, air conditioning and automatic food supply system which carries the blood on its repeated journey around the body. The centre of all these is the HEART.

The HEART never has a chance to rest. If it does the person will certainly die. Contracting at an average rate of about 70 beats a minute, it beats 4,200 times in an hour, 100,800 times a day. These figures add up to 36,792,000 times a year and a colossal 2,575,440,000 times in an average life time of 70 years. My heart never stops, never rests, and never complains. It is always happy to make me live and enjoy my life. I need to learn many things from my heart. My heart loves me so much so that the first moment when it beat, I became alive. If my heart had not beaten, I would never know what life is!

Just observing my heart can teach me a lot of wisdom. It never complains of too much work. It is consistently and patiently working 24/7 to keep me alive. Because of the constant working of my heart, all that I think, feel and do is possible. I can't thank my heart enough. The best way to express my gratitude to my heart is to live like my HEART - always working, always patient, always giving life.

- Be like your HEART!

81

My Sin of Omission

"Today, give a stranger one of your smiles. It might be the only sunshine he sees all day." **– Anonymous**

In life, there are many things that we take for granted. We don't bother all the people whom we encounter during each day. We never care to look at, smile or observe them. Why are we so apathetic towards others? Are we not of the same human family? Are they not a human being like us who need what you and I need? Why do we not try to understand another human person? Is it too burdensome to look at least one person and smile? These are simple acts but taken for granted. Even if a person is a stranger, I need to show my concern and respect. Many religions and cultures exhort its people to respect guests. Taittiriya Upanishad says, *"Atithi Devo Bhava"* (Guest is God). Jesus said in the Bible, *"I was a stranger and you invited me in."* *(Mt. 25:35).* I have come across the following story in a magazine I read some years back. I was so moved by this small incident. It taught me a great lesson not to take people for granted. It makes me realize that a human person needs to be treated with love and respect even if they are not known to me. The story runs thus:

> *"Last week a boy hanged himself from the roof of his father's barn. I used to watch him carrying water and feeding the goats as I passed by his gate, but never smile at him. I used to see him sitting and gazing at the lofty Kanchenjunga, but I didn't stop*

and tell him that I was a lover of nature too. When I heard that he was dead, I went with others to his house. Some said he was an orphan, others that he attended the night school. They told me that no one loved him. All the while I knew that I was his murderer. I killed him with my lack of care and concern."

I PROMISE TO... - Francois Krishnaire in *Friends*

- *Our responsibility in life is not only to perform our duty but to do all the good that we can do beyond our duty.*

82

My Weight is My Love

"A thought transfixed me: for the first time in my life I saw the truth as it is set into songs by so many poets, proclaimed as the final wisdom by so many thinkers. The truth – that is the ultimate and highest goal to which man can aspire. Then I grasped the meaning of the greatest secret that human poetry and human thought and belief have to impart; the salvation of man is through love and in love." **–Viktor Frankl in Man's Search for Meaning**

St. Augustine in his book "*The Confessions*" writes, "*My weight is my love: by it am I carried wheresoever I am carried*" (L. esferor quo cumque feror). A person has no bona fide inner weight without love. Therefore, love measures the true weight of a person. Love has an immeasurable weight. A person without love is like a vehicle without a steering. A person who loves love is being steered by love itself. He becomes a mere vehicle. He no longer controls or directs love but Love controls and directs him. Love carries him or her wherever it wants and desires. He or she just follows the promptings of love. The following is the difference between a human person and Love:

- A person may change but Love remains.
- A person may be fickle but Love is constant.
- A person is temporary but Love is permanent.
- A person loves passing objects but Love hates them for Love is eternal and wants everything eternal (I Corinth. 13:8).

A person never changes love but it is love which changes him. To follow the injunctions of love is a noble task and everyone who is guided by love transforms into a wonderful and beautiful human being. Subtract love in your life and you become nonentity.

83

Myopia

"We are all short-sighted, and very often see but one side of a matter, our views are not extended to all that has a connection with it. From this defect I think no man is free. We see but in part, and therefore, it is no wonder we conclude not right from our partial views."
– John Locke

Myopia is shortsightedness. Oculists say that it is brought on by always looking at objects that are near. So, it is good sometimes to go to the hill top and take a long view at the vast expanse of landscape. The Greek word from which myopia is derived can be translated as "cannot see far off." When we are shortsighted or myopic, we are not able to see the whole reality of things and thus, miss the truth. There is an interesting story of Galileo Galilei, an Italian astronomer, mathematician, physicist, philosopher and professor who made pioneering observations of the universe with long-lasting implications for the study of Physics. He was working hard to find evidence on the heliocentric claims of Corpernicus. In fact, with his discovery of the telescope, he had proven that Corpernicus's claims were true. His new found truth had now threatened to upset all theories those were previously held especially Ptolemy's geocentric theory which was in line with the biblical understanding of the motion of the planets. So, the whole Christendom opposed him. Galileo had requested one of the bishops, who was a member of the deadly Inquisition to see what he saw through his telescope but refused to look through. This shows the bishop was willfully blind and did not want to know the truth. This is the result of being short-sighted.

Those who are myopic can't see far objects. In real life, these are the people who look at every situation at the *prima facie* appearance. They look at only the surface and see only what is tangible and palpable and never beyond. They know only *what is happening* but they are not aware of *why it is happening. What is happening* is only symptomatic and superficial and *why it is happening* is a deeper insight of the situation. It is finding out the cause of the symptom. Shortsighted people see only the surface behaviour or action of a person but they have no idea why is the person behaving that way? or Why is he doing what he is doing? This second part of the question is important if we want to have a deeper understanding of people. A deeper insight will help us to understand and be sympathetic to people and their circumstances.

- *If you are myopic, you see only the surface.*
  If you are hypermetropic, you can see far into the depths beyond the surface.

84

No Longer Prepare to Fight

This is a true story of a British soldier which I have come across in the newspaper *Telegraph* (March 13, 2006). Ben Griffin, an SAS (Special Air Services) soldier refused to fight in Iraq and left the army over the illegal tactics of US troops and the policies of the coalition forces. Griffin was sent to Iraq and after three months of his stay in Baghdad he told his commander that he was no longer prepared to fight alongside American forces. He said he had witnessed *"dozens of illegal acts"* by US troops who viewed the Iraqis as *"untermenschen"* – the Nazi term for races regarded as sub-human. This was the first time that an SAS soldier refused to go into combat and quit the army on moral grounds. This decision of Griffin brought an end to his exemplary eight-year career in which he also served with the Parachute Regiment, taking part in operations in Northern Ireland, Macedonia and Afghanistan. Before Griffin, Flt. Lt. Malcolm Kendall-Smith, a Royal Air Force doctor had already refused to return to Iraq on grounds that the war is illegal.

Griffin who spent two years with the SAS said that the American military's "gung-ho and trigger-happy mentality" and tactics had completely undermined any chance of winning the hearts and minds of the Iraqi population. He also said that many innocent civilians were arrested in night-time raids and interrogated by American soldiers and most probably tortured.

Griffin eventually told SAS commanders at Hereford that he could not take part in a war which he regarded as "illegal". He added that the British Prime Minister and the government had repeatedly "lied" over the war's conduct.

Griffin expected that he would be labeled as a coward and would face a court martial and imprisonment after making what he described as *"the most difficult decision of my life."* Instead, he was discharged with a testimonial describing him as a *"balanced, honest, loyal and determined individual who possesses the strength of character to have the courage of his convictions."* Patrick Mercer, minister for homeland security said, "Trooper Griffin is a highly experienced soldier. This makes his decision particularly disturbing and his views and opinions must be listened to by the government."

Griffin is not only highly experienced, courageous and brave soldier but he is also a person who has the courage to stand for what he believes is the truth. He is a man with clear conscience and principles. Because of his high sense of ethics, he saw that what his friends did were morally wrong. Therefore, he decided to live by his convictions rather than compromised with the actions of his friends.

- *The majority of human beings live a conveniently compromised life instead of living out their convictions?*

85

Norfolk Island

This is a true story written as a preface to the book *"The Awesome power of Positive Thinking"* by John W. Drakeford, a professor of Counseling and Pastoral Psychology in South-Western Baptist Theological Seminary, Texas. The story runs thus: Norfolk Island must be one of the most beautiful spots in the world and is frequently called *"The Pacific Island Paradise"*. However, in its early days it was used by the British government as a penal settlement and the most incorrigible convicts were sent to this five-by-three-mile island for punishment. It became known by names like *"The Isle of Misery"*, *"The Hell Hole of the Pacific"* etc. On March 6, 1840, the ship *Nautilus* arrived at Norfolk Island with a notable passenger Captain Alexander Maconochie, who had come to run the infamous penal settlement. From Machonochie's previous experience, he had learned the futility of using force. He came to Norfolk Island with the original idea about how the penal colony should be run. Maconochie described the condition of the 1400 prisoners on Norfolk Island, "In every way their feelings were habitually outraged and their self-respect destroyed. For the "merest trifles" the convicts were flogged, ironed or confined for days on bread and water. They were fed more like hogs than man". This treatment had resulted in embittered, recalcitrant prisoners who became intractable as time went on. Maconochie's proposal was that the emphasis should be on reform rather than punishment. He proposed this idea be carried out by giving the convicts positive focused attention through his 'mark system'. He inaugurated the concept that "The fate of every man should be placed unreservedly in his own hands". An overseer of marks was appointed. For each good behaviour there was an allotment of marks and for each bad behaviour a debit of marks. It was possible through the mark system for a diligent convict to earn enough marks to cut his sentence in half. The act of entering the mark was itself an indication of attention to these people who felt they were completely without hope.

The fruit of the programme were seen in a landmark event that took place on Norfolk Island in celebration of late Queen Victoria's birthday on May 25, 1840. The gates of prison were thrown open and distinctions between guards and prisoners were forgotten for the day. All spent a memorable day mixing and mingling and attending theatrical performances presented by the convicts who showed themselves to have unusual dramatic ability during the event. Guards and prisoners sat and ate together.

Since, the traditional purpose of the penal system was punishment, Maconochie's immediate superior, Sir George Gibbs wrote to his superior Lord John Russel complaining about the crimes in handling the convicts. Russel in response gave instructions that Maconochie should be sent to another post and Norfolk Island went back to being the *Isle of Despair*.

After I read this story, I became so emotional. For those hopeless prisoners in the Norfolk Island, the arrival of a new captain may not be an exciting news as such, for they knew that every captain sent to this Island were not going to be soft to those heinous convicts. Their anxiety must have been whether this new captain would be same as the former ones or worse. In any case, they knew that no captain was going to be so considerate to them. As time passed by, this Captain seemed to be showing some signs of being different from the earlier captains. His ingenuity and creativity had given the prisoners a new way of looking at life. Their hopes began to simmer once again as the "mark system" was used for evaluating their performance. Those who performed well would find their sentence reduced to half. Once again, life was bustling with exhilaration and ebullience. But this was temporary as Captain Maconochie's immediate superior wrote a complaint against him to the higher superior and as a result, Maconochie had to be transferred and the Island was back to square one. The ending of this story is tragic and poignant. Sir George Gibbs is the one who made a complaint. He is a type, who could not see others happy and prospering. He acted as a killjoy for the prisoners. For the prisoners, Maconochie's presence in the Island was rarest of the rare event. They would never forget him in their lives. Everyone in life is called to give hope, joy and peace. If everyone knows this vocation in their life and practice it, then the despaired, and the hopeless can get a new lease of life.

A succinct analysis of the following characters:

- **Maconochie, Captain:** He is a person ready to abandon legalism, dogmatism and tradition, in order to facilitate the growth of the prisoners. He is of the view that at times it is necessary to break rules in order to help and make people prosper. He is open to change and is altruistic.
- **Sir George Gibbs,** (immediate superior): His attitude was that prisoners have to be treated like prisoners and not like free citizens. Convicts are convicts, not exonerates. Follow the status quo; not creating new rules. He is a conventionalist and traditionalist. Change is painful for him. Maintaining order is far better than inventing new strategies which can be at times risky. The welfare of others is not his concern but smooth maintenance of rules and regulations without any disturbance. Observance of strict rules is the only way to maintain peace. Rules are above everything.

- **Lord John Russel** (higher superior): He is a highly gullible person who easily believes what he hears. He is a person who wants short cuts to solutions. There is less room for assessment and evaluation. He acts with the first-thought and no room for second-thought. If he is humane, he would study the matter mention in the complaint. He would not accept information at face value. If he were concerned with the welfare of the prisoners, he would know that transferring of the captain was a tragic thing to do on his part.
- **Prisoners of Norfolk Island:** They are convicts who have no more hope of returning back home. Amidst hope against hope, Captain Maconochie's appearance in the scene brought a new hope. In him, they found a light at the end of the tunnel. The new captain once again brought new life amongst the prisoners. They found in him a potential hero who can change their fate. But all these abruptly ended as he was soon transferred at the complaint of his immediate superior.
- *When big elephants fight, the victims are innocent ants, grass and plants beneath which pay heavily in the process.*

86

Only Your Mind is Closed

"Try to keep your mind open to possibilities and your mouth closed on matters that you don't know about. Limit your 'always' and your 'nevers'."
– **Amy Poehler**

A wise king wanted advice about what to do when he faced a real crisis in his life. He met his master. The master gave him a locket and told him to open it only when he was in difficulty. After some years he was defeated in a battle and he lost his kingdom. He was worried, hopeless, dispirited and despondent and was hiding in a cave. He suddenly remembered what his master had told him. He opened the locket and there he found a note which said, "If one door closes, look for another door and if you find no door open, look for a window". He gained strength from this piece of advice and after a month won his kingdom back. He went to his master and thanked him and asked a question: "Master, why does the door close?"

"The door is always open, only your mind is closed," replied the master.

The mind can either create a bunch of opportunities or a great wall of limitation. It depends on how we use the mind. The mind is the greatest instrument that human beings possess. With it, he can create what he wants. The mind can either act as a great boon and a bane as well. The king after he got defeated saw no hope or avenues that will make him restore his kingdom or make his life prosper again. He was at the lowest ebb of his life, when he began to make use of his mind. His mind directed him to an event in the past. He remembered that his master had given him a locket and asked him to open only when he is in difficulty. He opened and found the words: "If one door closes, look for another door and if you find no door open, then look for a window". This word began to work in him. He realized that there is always an alternative way to solve a problem. By following such path, the king regained his kingdom.

From all these, what we see is that opportunity, success and defeat depend on the mind. It is how a person looks at it. The mind is ever creative and its power and energy can never be exhausted. The person who uses positively will find ways and opportunities to reap success. While, a person who uses negatively also will create ways that will lead to destruction. For a person who does not know how to use the mind, everything will be closed before him. He can't see opportunities or avenues for prosperity. For those who know how to use the mind, it is the greatest instrument for creating what one wants to be.

If you think you are beaten, you are
If you think you dare not, you don't,
If you like to win, but you think you can't
It is almost certain you won't.

If you think you'll lose, you're lost
For out of the world we find,
Success begins with a fellow's will
It's all in the state of mind.

If you think you are outclassed, you are
You've got to think high to rise,
You've got to be sure of yourself before
You can ever win a prize.

Life's battles don't always go
To the stronger or faster man,
But soon or late the man who wins
Is the man WHO THINKS HE CAN!

– Walter D. Wintle

- *Train your mind to work for you.*

87

Operate from the Heart, Not from the Mind

"My mind tells me to give up, but my heart won't let me."

– Lao Tzu

While the HEART is busy loving and caring, the MIND is busy reasoning and reflecting. When the heart sees a person in need, it at once galvanizes into action. But when the mind sees a person in need, it immediately reasons and says, "Is it right to help such a person or does he or she deserve? The Heart simply loves and cares without any condition and cunctation (delay). While, the MIND always operates with a second thought: "Should I help? Who is he? Does he deserve? Is it worth helping? Even if I help, how much? The MIND always calculates, measures, rationalizes, and inquires. It rarely acts. It wants to know only. It never passes beyond the boundary of cognition. The world of the HEART and the world of the MIND have a vast difference. The world of the HEART is governed by love, care, compassion, sympathy, empathy, peace, joy, and understanding. While, the world of the MIND is governed by scientific rationality, reflection, calculation, and measurement. The language construction of the world of the MIND is also different from that of the world of the HEART. Those who live in the world of the MIND are fond of using words like, why, how, what, when and where. Unless they used these interrogatives, they don't understand each other. The world of the MIND is the world of reflection, calculation, measurement, subtraction and addition. It is the world of mathematics, the world of reason and the world of hectic mental activity. Unless it is reasonable, it will not act or proceed in life. Those who live in this world are very able, acute, astute, brainy, brilliant, clever, canny, intellectual, perceptive, percipient, perspicacious, profound, quick, rational, sagacious, sensible, sharp, shrewd, smart, witty, trenchant and so on.

On the other hand, those who live in the world of the HEART communicate differently. The only language they use is the language of LOVE. Without using words, they understand each other. How nice it would be if we are able to understand each other without using words! i.e., without the person explaining himself/herself, I am able to understand him/her. The people who live in this world are not very clever, not intelligent, and not shrewd at all but they are very loving, affectionate, ardent, attached, caring, concerned, dear, devoted, fond, friendly, fatherly, motherly, brotherly, sisterly, inseparable, protective, tender, warm, genial, and amiable.

- *In which world do you live?*

88

Perseverance

"Let me tell you the secret that has led to my goal. My strength lies solely in my tenacity." **– Louis Pasteur**

Carlyle writes: "*Perseverance* is the very hinge of all virtues. On looking over the world, the *cause of nine-tenths of the lamentable failures* which occur in men's undertakings and darken and degrade so much of their history, lies not in *the want of talents* or the will to use them but in the *vacillating and desultory* mode of using them in *flying from object to object* in staring away at each little disgust and *thus applying the force* which might *conquer any one difficulty to a series of difficulties*, so large that no human force can conquer them. The *smallest brook* on earth, by *continuing to run* has hollowed out for itself a considerable valley to flow in. Commend me therefore to the virtue of perseverance. Without it all the rest are little better than fairy gold which glitters in your purse but when taken to market proves to be stale or cinders."

An analysis of Carlyle's statement:

(a) *"Virtue"*: Perseverance is one of the most important virtues of all virtues. Virtue refers to a good quality or habit. Therefore, virtue is a qualitative good which is indispensable for humane living. A person needs this virtue of perseverance if he wants to achieve noble goals in life.

(b) *"Cause... of the lamentable failures":* Most of our failures occur not because we do not possess talents but due to our *'vacillating and desultory'* manner of using them. In other words, people do not lack talents but they lack constancy and seriousness.

(c) *"Flying from object to object":* This is a clear sign of a vacillating mind (inconsistent mind). A fickle-minded person will never stick to anything for he has no clear goals. He will be like a butterfly that sits from one flower to another. He will be like a rolling stone that gathers no moss. Such person will end up achieving nothing.

(d) *"Thus, applying the force...to a series of difficulties":* This speaks about wrong channelization of one's energy. When we concentrate from object to object our energy is scattered. When there is no clear goal, our energy dissipates. Instead of applying our energy to a series of purposes, if we apply on one, just one purpose or goal we would have greater and sure chance of success.

(e) *"The smallest brook... continuing to run... hollowed out":* This is a metaphorical expression. We need to learn a lesson from the smallest stream. What lesson? *Continuing to run* i.e., it never stops running. It goes on flowing and as a result it hollows out its way through the valley to flow. Because of its continuous, consistent and persistent flow it is able to make its own course in the valley though it is a small stream. There is a Latin phrase which says,

"Gutta cavat lapidem" which means 'a drop hollows a stone'. In the same way if we continuously, consistently and persistently work on our latent talents and abilities, one day our effort will be crown with success. Like the smallest brook if we continue in our efforts to improve our abilities without giving up, one day we will be able to make and create our own course in life.

89

Prejudice

"Prejudice is the child of ignorance." — **William Hazlitt**

I would define Prejudice as *"an already arranged or fixed idea before knowing what the actual reality is."* It is an attitude or world-view that is characterized by insufficient knowledge and information about a reality. Prejudice is believing an unverified information (rumour or hearsay) as true and factual. It is a fossilized presumption about the reality based on inadequate information or unverifiable intuition. It is a non-possession of adequate information about the reality. Prejudice has therefore, the potentiality to mar one's attitude to a frazzle. It is one of the greatest impediments to mature thinking and objective reasoning. It is the number one culprit that bars the way to an intelligent and logical structuring of one's personal thought. Prejudice fatally affects a person's world-view. Once prejudice has gone deep into a person, such person can never be objective in his judgment. His assessment of things will always go awry. A prejudice mind always makes *a shot in the dark* i.e. without proper knowledge of the reality, one passes judgment blindly and a person takes this judgment as the whole truth about the reality. This judgment may be either true or false. It is highly probable. Probability is never the truth. It is only a half-baked conjecture. If a person wants to be sound in knowing the reality, he cannot base his judgment and attitude on probable imperatives like *"may be"* or *"can be"* because such probable imperatives have no foundation and can never lead to the truth. Prejudice is proto-enemy of truth (reality). The human MIND is the seat of prejudice. Therefore, any error in the mind's perception affects the attitude of a person. The mind is highly receptive, perceptive, keen and sharp. It instantly receives any given data. Every moment, the human mind receives an innumerable data. The sources of these data can be friends, parents, brothers and sisters, ancestors, teachers, mass media and so on. These data are translated in the form of ideas and information. These ideas and information are not yet purified or refined. Every individual views the reality from the angle of their subjective prism. There is always an element of biasness in their world-view. Every individual mind therefore, has the responsibility to process, analyze, dissect and select these data. In other words, it has to go through the process of sieving or filtering. Otherwise it can negatively impact the attitude and thought structure of a person.

The mind which does not take the trouble of going through the process of filtering or purification will soon be fraught with prejudice. When I get a report that somebody is a dipsomaniac or a floozy, my mind receives this piece of information which may or may not be true. But it is my duty to process, analyze and find out the reality. If I am only a gullible recipient and not an analyst of ideas and information, then, instantly I will consume those information and conclude them as the truth. When I continuously hold on to this subjectively concluded idea, it gets transformed into prejudice. I will therefore, be easily infected by prejudice for all ideas and information do not come in a purified form. One should possess an *"Interrogative Psyche"* i.e. a *Questioning Mind*. When a person receives any idea or information, one must at once interrogate and establish its reliability and validity; only then, accept it. This constant practice will keep one's mind pure, refined and authentic. This is a mind free from prejudice.

90

Presumption

"The only barrier to truth is the presumption that you already have it."
– Chuck Missler

If we gaze meticulously into our cognitive configuration or the contours of our minds, we will find a combo of ideas and opinions on things and persons. If we observe intently and minutely, we will further recognize that our minds are not able to deliver objective opinions most of the time. This is the borderline where presumption takes over and controls us. Presumptions are not facts; they are based on an awry principle of *"may be"*. They are not imperative but relative. It is not a reliable source of knowledge and information. People who are presumptive possess high degree of prejudice. Presumption is one of the chief sources of prejudice and suspicion. Sometimes, we presume that Mr. X is good, and Mr. Y is bad; A is agreeable and B is disagreeable; C is a friend and D is a foe. We presume things like these, without verifying. How do we presume? Most of our presumptions are the result of unfiltered information (message that I get from people or any other sources) by which one forms personal opinion without any verification or sufficient evidence. People who consume information directly without filtering will be very presumptive and highly prejudiced. So, the best way to get rid of presumption is not to consume any information or to form any opinion without sufficient reason. This will help you to assess yourself and others more accurately.

In ancient Greece, Socrates the famous Greek philosopher was once visited by his acquaintance who was so eager to share a gossip. The man asked Socrates if he would like to know the story he had just heard about a friend of theirs. Socrates replied that before the man spoke, he needed to pass the "Triple- Filter Test".

The first filter, he explained is Truth.

"Have you made absolutely sure that what you are about to say is true?"

The man shook his head. "No, I actually just heard about it, and..."

Socrates cut him off.

"You don't know for certain that it is true, then.

"Is what you want to say something good or kind?" Again, the man shook his head. "No! actually, just the opposite. You see ..."

Socrates lifted his hand to stop the man speaking.

"So, you are not certain that what you want to say is true and it isn't good or kind. One filter still remains, though, so you may yet still tell me.

That is Usefulness or Necessity. Is this information useful or necessary to me?"

A little defeated, the man replied, "No, not really."

"Well, then, "Socrates said, turning on his heel. "If what you want to say is neither true, nor good or kind, nor useful or necessary, please don't say anything at all."

This anecdote teaches us not to consume any information without filtering. It teaches us not to pay attention to rumours, gossip or any unfounded message from any source. Socrates' Triple Filter Truth is a very good method for overcoming our propensity to presume things. It is always good to apply this

Triple-Filter Truth by asking ourselves before we voice our opinion:

- Is it true?
- Is it good?
- Is it kind?
- Is it useful?
- Is it necessary?

91

Purity

"Blessed are the pure in heart; they shall see God." – **Bible**

Zoologists eulogize the beautiful behaviour of an Ermine animal. The Ermine animal is a little animal found in the forests of northern Europe and Asia. Its snow-white fur is sold in the fur markets of the world and in many places, is seen as a symbol of purity. In some countries, the hunters take cruel advantage of the ermine's care to keep its fur clean. After finding its home which may be a cleft in the rock or the hollow of a tree, they daub the entrance and the interior with filth. Then their dogs are let loose to chase the little animal. Frightened by them the ermine runs to take refuge in its home but finding it daub with filth, it refuses to go in and spoil its pure white coat. It prefers to die in the claws of the yelping dogs rather than spoil the purity of its fur.

Ermine's story is very inspiring indeed. This animal is ready to give up its life than soil it. The Bible says, *"Blessed are the pure in heart; they shall see God"* (Mt.5:8). Purity is a virtue that is highly valued in many religions. The Bible says that only the *'pure in heart'* shall see God; if that is the case, then, I think there is no heart which is completely pure. Thus, there is no one who can see God. Literally speaking, there is no heart which is totally pure. Then, what does *'pure in heart'* in the Bible mean? If we look closely and observe:

- A PURE HEART is not a perfect condition. It is a heart that has known and experienced suffering and sorrow, pain, anger, happiness, loneliness and so on. It has cracks and scars on it. It is not innocent but has a lot of experiences. It has become strong, firm, steady and reliable through experience.
- A PURE HEART is a heart filled with love. It is always ready to pour its love without ceasing no matter how painful and broken it is.
- A PURE HEART always listens and shows genuine care and empathy to the people around it.
- A PURE HEART is a heart filled with magnanimity. It spontaneously gives what it has and never expects anything in return.
- A PURE HEART is a heart that readily forgives and is forgiven. It harbours no hurts or bitterness.
- A PURE HEART is a heart filled with joy. It happily gives joy to others and enjoys the presence of others.
- A PURE HEART is a heart that is genuinely hospitable and has no limit in welcoming others, it opens its doors always for those who are in need. Since, its doors are always opened, some take advantage, yet, it welcomes them.
- A PURE HEART is a heart that sometimes gets mistreated or misunderstood because of its overflowing kindness and benevolence.

Only this type of PURE HEART will see God.

- *Every person has the capacity to create a pure heart.*

92

Ready a Child to Face Life

The greatest gift that one can give to a child is to train him or her in the art of facing life, for life is the greatest odd that every person has to encounter. W.B. Yeats in his poem *"A Prayer For My Daughter,"* pictures his innocent babe in the cradle, beset with the howling storm outside, which is the pre-figuration of the trials and troubles in the real world, awaiting the entry of the new creature into the arena of life. The new child does not know that she is being waited by the howling storm (sufferings of life). The child is living in innocence and ignorance. The child is not aware of the howling storm that is just waiting to swallow her. This is what happens to every new life that has come into the world. Therefore, it is a gargantuan task for parents and teachers to train a child in the art of facing the odds of life. Life is not easy to live at times. It is not always a bed of roses. At times, it can be so harsh that a person can lose hope and feel meaningless. Therefore, to face life, one should be made of a sterner stuff otherwise, one will have to perish in the fight. In such battle, only the brave and courageous will survive. When the going gets tough, it is common for a person to stop seeing one's strengths and only focus on one's weaknesses. Such person will see himself or herself as a loser, incapable of rising above tough situations. But this should not happen. Every human person is a combination of strengths and weaknesses. Therefore, the key is to remind oneself that one has lots of strengths. Try to remember some of your strengths in particular or do a quick mental check of some of your strengths. By doing this mental exercise, your perception of yourself will change and this will empower you and give you confidence that you can handle effectively the situation you're in. Dwelling on your problems makes your situation worse. Always thinking of what you don't want, works against what you do want. If you have overcome a difficult situation in your life, it will give you the confidence to overcome the next difficult situation too. What is important is, to learn at least one lesson from every difficult situation. This will make you more wise and gradually, you will learn how to handle any situation in life.

So, to face the stark realities of life, one must make oneself fit. Childhood is thus, the most ideal time to begin to prepare the child in the art of facing life. The child's mind and body are supple and susceptible. It easily imbibes any given data. The best data that can be imprinted in the child's mind is knowledge of life's realities, the patience to bear, the courage to face them and hope to overcome them.

- *We shall overcome*
  We shall overcome
  We shall overcome someday...

93

Search for Something Eternal

"What comes easy won't last. What lasts won't come easy."

– Unknown

Gautama Buddha was born and brought up in the lap of luxury. He never knew what despair was for he was surrounded and attended constantly by a band of happy people who were selected by the king, who wanted to hide unhappiness from his son from the day Siddhartha was born. His father ordered the meticulous protection of the young Siddhartha within the gamut of the palace from the hard realities of life. The young boy was not allowed to see anything that dies and decays e.g. decaying flowers, dead leaves, ugly and old people for all these can cause despair in him. The intention of the king was to protect his son from anything that could cause unhappiness or any emotional disturbance. But as the boy grew up, one day, he wanted to see the town and that could not be refused by the king because saying "no" to what the young prince wanted could emotionally disturb him. So, the charioteer was asked to take the young prince and show him the town. Up to now, the princess didn't know what is sadness, frustration, despair, old age, death, decay etc., because all these were hidden from him in the palace.

A princess who was meticulously protected from all miseries of life took a different turn on the day he was driven into the city by his charioteer. First, he saw an old man coughing and double bent. He asked his charioteer, "What has happened to this man?" The charioteer said, "This is called old age and it happens to everybody". And immediately he said, "Is it going to happen to me too?" The charioteer said, "I feel bad saying it, but I cannot say untruth. You are not excluded. It is going to happen to you too." This was the first-time young Siddhartha saw an old man. Then, the young Buddha was totally overcome by despair for the first time in his life. So far, he saw only beautiful and happy girls, fresh flowers, music, dances, wine etc. At the next moment, he saw a dead body being carried and some people weeping. Now, this was the first time he was seeing a death person which he didn't understand yet. He didn't know what death was! He asked his charioteer, "What has happened to this man and why is he being carried?" the charioteer told him, "This is the second stage after the first one that you've seen just now. After that one dies." Buddha asked, "Is this too going to happen to me?" As they were engaged in confabulation another man came in with a beautiful red robe, a radiant face, a tremendous aura around him – a sannyasin. Buddha asked, "Who is this man?" His charioteer said, "This man is a sannyasin. He became aware of the realities of life that human existence is going to disappear into old age, old age will lead into death, and death to the funeral pyre; so, he has given up everything in order to search for deathlessness."

All these experiences woke him up from his ignorant slumber. His experience in the town was completely haunting his mind. He was interiorly disturbed. Therefore, he decided to depart from the world and went into silence in search of something which is deathless and eternal that will be beyond death and decay. He declared that he would not rest for a single moment until he would find deathlessness and eternal-ness. To find this he went from one sannyasin to another but finally found that they could not help him. So, he went to himself. Here, he started the inward journey within himself. He retired himself into silence and finally he was enlightened i.e. all ignorance have ceased and light began to dawn upon him. He had already found deathlessness.

For most people, the experience of superficial physical beauty is the ne plus ultra of happiness. If this physical pulchritude could give eternal bliss, then why should Buddha leave the royal palace, where all the physical beauties and comforts of life were all at his disposal? He left all of them for he knew that all these physical beauties of life are passing and anything that passes does not last and anything that does not last, dies and anything that dies comes to nothing. Therefore, what is pertinent here is: Are you striving after nothing? It is better to strive for something deathless and eternal. You can find this only if you are willing to encounter yourself. Retire into silence and walk down or go deeper into yourself and begin eliminating ignorance (evil) and after ignorance is conquered, light will dawn upon you. When light dawns upon you, then you are already in the state of deathlessness and eternalness. You are the *TATHAGATA* (beyond all transitory phenomena). You have attained light for light is eternal and to be in the light is bliss. Whereas, darkness is not eternal for as soon as light appears, it disappears. Jesus said, "I am the light of the world"

(Jn. 8:12).

94

Sibling Relationship

> *"A person who is there when you need him; someone who picks you up when you fall; a person who sticks up for you when no one else will; a brother is always a friend. Nothing can stop me from loving my brother."* **– Unknown**

Once there were two brothers who used to quarrel and fight every day in the family. As the sibling rivalry continued, their animosity too increased and gradually the conflict became chronic. Their father would advise them, time and again, not to fight and sometimes punished them but to no avail. They could no longer live together, eat together and work together. Whenever they were together, they would start fighting. Their father and the other family members became more and more worried because if the two brothers continue in their antagonism, they could kill each other one day.

One fateful morning as the family members were getting ready to eat their morning meal, their Daddy stood up and began to admonish lovingly to all his children including the two brothers:

> *"Dear children! We are now about to eat our morning meal. Before we eat, I would like to say something very important to you all. There is an old adage that says, 'Morning meal is a parting meal and evening meal is a get-together meal'. So, let us know that every morning meal is a parting meal because*

after this meal, we all will be going for our own daily duties and works; we do not know what will happen to each of us during the day. Anything can happen to any of us – sickness, accident, or any calamity. When the time comes for evening meal, we do not know whether all of us will be there to eat together. We are not sure whether our evening meal will be a get- together meal! Therefore, let us love and forgive one another; shun all hatred and hostility towards one another and share this meal with love."

Their father had not yet finished speaking, when the two brothers started fighting. The elder brother hit hard on the face of his younger brother and he fell instantly on the floor and his nose began to bleed profusely. The younger brother was so deeply hurt that without eating the meal that morning he ran away from the house. Nobody knew where he went. That afternoon their father got a phone call telling him that his son had just died of an accident; knocked down by a vehicle on the road. The family was completely shocked to hear the news. The father rushed to the accident site and found that his son committed suicide by jumping into the oncoming vehicle. When the elder brother came to know the news of his brother's death, he cried inconsolably filled with terrible guilt and remorse and said to himself, "If I were to listen to my father's advice this morning, my brother would not have committed suicide. It was I who turned out my own brother from the house and I am the one who kill him".

Let us learn to listen to the advice of our parents and elders. If we listen to their advice, we will seldom regret in life. This is because they always advice for our good. Today, many children label their parents as "knowing nothing" may be they are not tech savvy (ignorant in terms of handling the modern technology and gadgets) as we are in the age of technology but when it comes to the realities of life (experience) they have better and richer experience. They know what life is better than anyone else. So, listening to them will greatly help us to meet the challenges of life in a better manner. We may have misunderstanding, conflicts, and differences in opinions and sometimes even serious fights in the family but let us not forget to forgive. Let us learn to forgive and be compassionate to our family members, neighbours and others. Let us not regret in life because of our own laxity and sloppiness. Those who practice love, compassion, forgiveness, and humility never regret in life.

- *If you don't love on time; you will sink into guilt sooner or later.*

95

Sloth, The Devil Within

"Laziness is a secret ingredient that goes into failure. But it's only kept a secret from the person who fails." – **Robert Half**

A man had many sons and all of them turn out to be downright lazybones and slugabeds. They never knew the words 'work', 'struggle', and 'effort'. They seemed to be the most indolent and lethargic coterie of brothers that ever lived. One day their father could no longer compromise with their goings-on. Their father wanted to find out who was the laziest among his sons. So, with his stentorian voice he blasted, "Listen! My dear sons, today there is going to be a '*Sloth Competition*' in our family and the winner will be given a handsome prize". The youngest son from his cozy bed answered in a dull fading voice, "Dad! I am sorry, I will not be able to attend the competition". And he won the championship.

Sloth is both physical and mental disease that stings the larger population of our society. All want to gain and profit without lifting a finger. All want to receive and nobody wants to work. All want to be fed and nobody wants to feed. All want to sit and nobody wants to stand. All are stung by the asp of idleness. Most of our existential problems can be solved if every person by his or her own free will chooses to work. Then, our world would be a better, richer, wealthier and more prosperous place to live in. Lazy people are the most cunning people in the world.

The reason is that since they don't want to work, they use their brain in order to survive. The brain is active 24/7 in order to hatch the best ideas on how to get or earn without spending an iota of their energy. Such people use their brain negatively and as a result they become clever, shrewd, cunning and crafty. Their words are sweet and they can convince simple people easily. Imam Ali says, "*The cheater has a sweet tongue and a bitter heart*". Don't be fooled by a sweet talker. Believe someone whose actions and mouth speak at the same thing. This is how we identify, a cheater or a lazy person. Bill Gates says, "*I choose a lazy person to do a hard job. Because a lazy person will find an easy way to do it.*" They are cunning so, they know short cuts to complete a job without spending much energy.

The old hackneyed proverb says, "An idle man's brain is devil's workshop". Once the door of an idle man's mind is open, the devil will enter and start disseminating its propaganda. Then, he becomes an apprentice to the devil and finally becomes *Advocatus Diaboli* (spokesperson of the devil) and starts defending the devil in his thoughts, words and actions. He speaks and defends the devil everywhere. He becomes *alter Diabolus* (another Devil). Keep this dictum of St. Jerome in mind: "*Fac et aliquid operis ut semper te diabolus inveniat occupatum*" (Do something so that the devil may find you busy).

- *Shun laziness and begin to work. Those who work, get what they need and those who work harder, get what they want.*

96

Sub-Inspector's Heroism

"No one is actually dead until the ripples they cause in the world die away." – **Unknown**

The Reader Digest reported a very poignant incident of the sacrifice of Sub Inspector Sanjeev Kumar during the great Tsunami of 2004. This took place at Katchal in Andaman and Nicobar Islands. Deepika was watching her husband Sanjeev Kumar braved waters once, twice... four times, each time returning with a rescued neighbour. After he had rescued four, Sanjeev saw an elderly woman, a hundred metres away, screaming for help. By now the water level had risen dangerously. Sanjeev recognised the woman. "Let me go and save her," Sanjeev told Deepika. "She used to feed me long back when I had just moved in here. She's like my mother." Sanjeev swam to the woman. Deepika watched as he then carried her for about 25 metres towards the temple. Just then a second giant wave struck. Sanjeev grabbed a coconut palm with one hand and held on to the woman with his other hand. Deepika started running down towards Sanjeev. "My husband shouted back at the four others he'd rescued to stop me from running into the water," recalls Deepika who soon lost sight of Sanjeev.

Although the sub-inspector's body was never found, Deepika received a silver medallion from the Islands' lieutenant-governor citing Sanjeev's *"devotion to duty during Tsunami."* Sanjeev died but he saved lives. The greatest and most precious gift in life is life itself. But to let go one's own existence for a greater cause is the noblest of all things. It is reality that some people live their lives meaningfully for a cause, while others end up in futility. The meaning of life is discovered when a person is able to get clarity on one's life purpose and pursues that to the point of sacrificing everything including life itself. He forges ahead once he is certain that he is on a path of a cause that is worth dying for. Jesus had such experience. He had a complete clarity on his life's purpose and pursued to accomplish his mission to the point of sacrificing his life. In the Bible says, *"Greater love has no one than this: to lay down one's life for one's friends"* (John 15:13). Jesus taught that giving up one's life for the sake of someone is the greatest love one can show to a person. So, what is important in life is identifying and persistently pursuing a cause worth dying for! Ernest Hemingway says, *"Every man's life ends the same way. It is only the details of how he lived and how he died that distinguish one man from another."*

- *All great people in history had sacrificed their lives for others.*

97

Suffering is a Great Teacher

"Out of suffering have emerged the strongest souls; the most massive characters are seamed with scars." **– E.H. Chapin**

Suffering is part and parcel of our existential fabric. It is a multifaceted reality and takes multifarious forms and appearances. It constantly changes its appearances. It takes the form of illness, hurt, pain, death, anguish, dejection, despair, frustration, hopelessness, depression and the list goes on. Suffering is truly a troublesome trouble, a problematic problem, yet, it is really real. It comes like a thief and steals away one's peace and joy. It is a killjoy and a wet blanket. It is ingrained in the fabric of human existence and therefore, ineluctable. It has to be met with nerve and valour. Never run away from it for there is no escape. Instead welcome it into your life as a friend and teacher from whom you can learn and draw lessons of life. Remember, a suffering understood is a fountain forever. Welcome it as your benevolent teacher, just as a prepared student is happy to meet his teacher and not like an unprepared student who is always fear-stricken and trying to escape at the sight of his teacher. For an unprepared student, the teacher becomes an object of fear, burden and trouble. So, prepare to meet any suffering in life. Every suffering should teach us at least one lesson. If we consider suffering as a great teacher, we can draw great inspirations of life and it can be a perennial fountain. DMX, an American rapper, songwriter and actor quoting Nietzche in his 1998 song "Slippin" gives us a beautiful reflection on suffering - to find meaning in suffering.

> *"To live is to suffer.*
>
> *To survive, well, that's to find meaning in the suffering."* Nietzche famously remarked that what doesn't kill us make us stronger. Wisdom emerges from suffering. When things go well in life, we don't bother to reflect or examine our lives. But when we face a difficult situation, we begin to reflect on how to face it or how to overcome it. Finally, reflecting on our experiences give us new lessons in the form of wisdom which will help us in the future. Khenchen Konchog Gyaltshen Rinpoche, the Tibetan monk speaks about four benefits of suffering - wisdom, resilience, compassion, and a deep respect for reality.

Let us analyze the character of Robinson Crusoe, the hero of the novel *Robinson Crusoe* by John Bunyan. Suffering put Crusoe in a catch 22 and fixed him in a hopeless miasma of depression but he was finally able to surmount his situation. It was on September 30, 1659 that Crusoe was shipwrecked during a dreadful storm and in the offing came on shore on the dismal unfortunate island which he called the "Island of Despair", all the rest of the ship's company were drowned and only he was saved. All the rest of that day he spent in afflicting himself at the dismal circumstance he was brought to, namely, he had neither food, house, clothes, weapon or place to fly to, and in despair of any relief, saw nothing but death before him, either that he should be devoured by wild beasts, murdered by savages or starved to death for want of food. At the approach of night, he slept on a tree for fear of wild creatures but slept soundly though it rained all night. In spite of all the miseries, Robinson Crusoe started reflecting and finally found that heaven was upon him. He realized that amidst such catastrophe, God had preserved only his life, as all his companions perished. He considered this as the greatest blessing showered upon him by God.

The sufferings of Crusoe in the "*Island of Despair*" were beyond measure. There were times in which he was in bitter sorrow but he faced his problems and pain boldly. Suffering taught him great lessons during his life in the island. He learned to trap animals and tamed them for his purpose. He learned how to raise crops, how to build a house and he learned the laws of jungle. At the end he was contented and happy living alone in the island. He finally found the reward of suffering which made him a harder man. Thenceforth, he was able to meet any situation. Crusoe is the man who reaps the fruits of suffering.

- *Sufferings have come into our lives to teach us a new way of looking at reality.*

98

Tell the Truth

"Honesty is more than lying. It is truth telling, truth speaking, truth living and truth loving." **– Faust**

It is very difficult to tell the truth in a society where lie is worshipped as god. Today, lie is being worshipped as a deity in a corruption-stricken society. People in general tell lies readily than truth because it is lucrative, convenient, and advantageous and averts troubles. So, lie is thriving and prospering because it has found a fertile ground to grow. It has become a huge monster that appears to be invincible. Since, the majority of the people in the society are infected by this malaise, there is no one who has the courage to fight against this monster. When the powerful and the elite have used this as an instrument to further their cause, nobody dares to expose this monster. Lie is the greatest enemy of truth. But those who speak and practice the truth are only a miniscule minority and seems to be voiceless. Since, there is no one to bell the cat, this monster has grown oversize becoming more and more powerful and dictating everyone. People today have conveniently accepted its inunctions which they find so lucrative. Practicing lie has become a way of life.

One of the ways one can counter lie is, to practice the truth fearlessly and consistently. This is the only way to counter lies. It is the duty of every individual to spy out lies and bring it to the light. This is a thankless and dangerous job but a noble enterprise. M.N. Roy, one of the greatest Indian thinkers of the 20th century writes, *"Lie hunting is my profession. This is a thankless job. But someone must tell the truth, if it is not to remain an empty concept. I've been lie-hunting ever since I learn to think for myself to distinguish facts from fictions. It has not won me popularity."* Lie hunting should become one's profession. This is a hard and unrewarding job. Many will not appreciate you for this job because they are living on the benefits brought in by lies and corruption. What is happening today is that a few people are being hunted for hunting lies. Telling the truth directly exposes and hurts liars and this is a very dangerous venture. The hunter becomes the hunted. But because of the risks and dangers, one should not stop practicing the truth. One should not allow fear to control him. It is better to die practicing the truth than live one's life fraught with lies. A person who lives in the truth is bound to be hated in a lie and corruption-stricken society.

When Swami Vivekananda was a small boy his mother told him, *".... Always follow the truth, without caring about the result. Very often you may've to suffer injustice or unpleasant consequences for holding the truth but you must not under any circumstances abandon it."* In order to tell the truth and to be heard one should be within the truth as Michel Foucault says, *"It is never enough simply to speak the 'truth' if one wishes to be heard; one must be 'within' the 'truth' and embody its 'regime.'"* Only the person who has the ability to discern truth from falsehood is entitled to give a verdict concerning the validation of any issue. Descartes, the father and originator of modern philosophy once said, *"I have always had an extreme desire to learn how to distinguish the true from the false, in order to see clearly how I should act and to be able to travel with the assurance through this life."*

You are a passer-by in this world and as you're travelling along, you'll find your path strewn with lies, falsehood, corruption and so on. Therefore, it is your bounden duty to constantly tell others and yourself about the truth. When you fight valiantly against falsehood then, your journey will become an expedition and an adventure and finally, when you reach your destination, you'll be filled with great joy and happiness. And looking back your journey, you'll have the satisfaction of telling yourself: *"I have told the truth and I have chosen the path which was less travelled by"*.

99

The Character of Gabriel Oak (Farmer Oak)

(A character from the novel *Far From the Madding Crowd*)

In my study of English literature, I had always enjoyed how the author creates and develops the different characters in the drama or novel. Characterization is one of the most complex and intricate work of many good writers which requires a deep peep into human nature. Characterization always fascinated me during my graduation and post graduate studies in English literature. I was particularly attracted by the different characters presented in the literary dramas, novels and fictions. In my study of the novel *"Far From the Madding Crowd"* by Thomas Hardy, I was so much enamoured by the character of Gabriel Oak. He is an epitome and representative of many human beings. He represents the character of the majority of the people living in our age. This is why I pick up to study this man's character. By studying Gabriel Oak many of us can understand our own personalities and be transformed.

When Farmer Oak smiled, the corners of his mouth spread till they were within an unimportant distance of his ears, his eyes were reduced to chinks and diverging wrinkles appeared round them, extending upon his countenance like the rays in a rudimentary sketch of the rising sun. His Christian name was Gabriel and on working days he was *a young man of sound judgment*, *easy motions*, *proper dress* and *general good character*. *On Sundays he was a man of misty views*, rather *given to postponing*, and hampered by his best clothes and umbrella: upon the whole, one who felt himself to occupy morally that vast middle space of *Laodicean neutrality* which lay *between the communion people of the parish and the drunken section* – that is, he went to church but yawned privately by the time the congregation reached the Nicene creed, and *thought of what there would be for dinner when he meant to be listening to the sermon*. Or, to state *his character as it stood in the scale of public opinion, when his friends and critics were in tantrums, he was considered rather a bad man; when they were pleased, he was rather a good man;* when they were neither, he was a man whose moral colour was *a kind of pepper-and-salt mixture.*

Since he lived six times as many working days as Sundays, Oak's appearance in his old clothes was most peculiarly his own – *the mental picture formed by his neighbours in imagining him always dressed in that way*. He wore a low-crowned felt hat, spread out at the base by tight jamming upon the head for the security in high winds and a coat like Dr. Johnson's; his lower extremities being encased in ordinary leather leggings and boots emphatically large, affording to each foot a roomy apartment so constructed that any wearer might stand in a river all day long and know nothing of damp – their maker being a conscientious man who endeavoured to compensate for any weakness in his cut by unstinted dimension and solidity.

Mr. Oak carried about him, by way of watch, what may be called a small silver clock; in other words, it was a watch as to shape and intention and a small clock as to size. This instrument being *several years older than Oak's grandfather* and had the peculiarity of going either too fast or not at all... Oak had just reached the time of life at which 'young' is ceasing to be the prefix of 'man' in speaking of one. He was at the brightest period of masculine growth, for *his intellect and his emotions were clearly separated: he had passed the time* during which the influence of youth indiscriminately mingles them in the character of impulse and *he had not yet arrived at the stage wherein they become united again* in the character of prejudice, by the influence of a wife and family. In short, he was 28 and a bachelor. The field he was in the morning sloped to the ridge called Norcombe Hill.

Analysis of the Character of Gabriel Oak:

(a) *"... a young man of sound judgment":* Gabriel Oak was a young man with a good sense of judgment. He is able to analyze situations and events correctly which many people are not capable of.

(b) *"easy motions":* Oak is not a complex character. He acts and conducts himself without much effort. In other words, he easily acts without much seriousness, thoughtfulness and less tension. Without any complexity he acts spontaneously.

(c) *"proper dress":* He is a person of decent appearance. He is a man of average fashion who wants to appear before others decently but not too smart.

(d) *"general good character":* This is the aggregate assessment of his character *generally good in character.* That means he was neither a bad character nor very illustrious. He was in a way just good. Good is the base for better and best. There is a room for a big improvement. He has not become better and still far from best. That means he has not excelled anyone in his character. He is in a way just above bad. He belongs to a common character of the general people.

(e) *"On Sundays he was a man of misty views"*: As a Christian, he is to observe Sunday as a holy day and he should be fervent and religious and clear in his conscience and he is to actively participate in the Church's service. But instead of being fervent and active he is not clear about his Sunday observances. True, he goes to the church but it seems to be just a duty and not religiosity. So, *"he went to church but yawned privately by the time the congregation reached the Nicene Creed"*. This is a clear sign of passive attendance. Though he is passive in the church, he is still better than those who don't attend the church at all. This is how "just good" people behave. At least we appreciate him for fulfilling his duty. There are many people who just perform their duty and not more. But according to the rating of the author, he is *"between the communion people of the parish and the drunken section"*. That means he is a little better than the drunken section of the society and lower than the communion people (who lived a holy and good Christian life) of the parish.

(f) *"given to postponing":* He is a person of tomorrow and not today. He is a person who does not want to struggle at the moment but afterwards. But we do not know that afterwards is a reality for him because he is a man who postpones. Most people have this type of character. They don't want to struggle at the moment and would postpone or delay. They want to relax at the present moment. Postponement or procrastination is an unhealthy sign of good character. Another name for postponement is laziness. This is a clear indication of a weak character. This kind of character seldom accomplish or succeed in life.

(g) *"thought of what there would be for dinner when he meant to be listening to the sermon":* Here, Oak's character contains the elements of anticipated worry, hypocrisy, pretense, confusion and distraction. He is worried about his dinner. His hypocrisy and pretense is that he acts as if he is listening to the sermon when his thoughts are on the dinner. He does something and thought of another thing. His distraction has caused a rift between his body and mind. The dichotomy in his character is clearly seen when his physical body is present in the church but his mind and spirit are absent. When there is no coordination between the body, mind and spirit, this is a sign that there is confusion within the person. This kind of people lack coordination and integrity in life. This is what happens to people of 'generally good' character.

(h) *"Laodicean neutrality":* The word "Laodicean" means indifferent or lukewarm in matters of religion. Oak was a person who was neutral regarding religion and piety. He was neither cold nor hot in his religiosity. He was just lukewarm. He practices his religious obligations but not too seriously. Just duty for duty's sake. Today, this is a disease that is affecting many people. Many people don't deny God but they are just indifferent. Due to this "the falcon cannot hear the Falconer..." says W.B. Yeats. Many are trapped in the *Laodicean neutrality.*

(i) *"his character as it stood in the scale of public opinion, when his friends and critics were in tantrums, he was considered rather a bad man; when they were pleased, he was rather a good man":* Oak's character is like a palindrome i.e., which can be read backward or forward. People can read him from any side, that is when his friends were not happy with him, he was considered as a bad person and when they are pleased with him, he is considered a good person. He is an exploited and manipulated character. His character and reputation depends on others. His character is alterable according to the whims and fancies of his friends and critics. This is a clear sign of a frail and fragile character.

(j) *"the mental picture formed by his neighbours in imagining him always dressed in that way":* Oak is a person known by his neighbours thoroughly. Their mental picture was *"always...that way"*. Always... that way shows that Oak was predictable not only in dress but in his character too. His neighbours were able to interpret him. This is dangerous in life. A person who knows you thoroughly sometimes can take advantage of you and he is sure to say, "I know this person" and he also can play with your life. Once people can read you through and through, you are highly susceptible to their manipulation. Therefore, never allow others to know you through and through. Of course, they need to know something about you but not everything. Everything is not required. Maintain a 'mystery' in your life which others cannot interpret or have access. This will create a fear in them that they are not able to understand you completely. Manipulation takes place only when people know you completely.

(k) *"This instrument being several years older than Oak's grandfather"*: Oak has a sense of traditionalism. It is good to preserve things of old. Oak did not merely inherit the old watch from his grandfather and great- grandfathers but also their generosity and love. There are so many good things (values) we inherit from our grandparents, great-grandparents and parents, we should preserve them and hand them over to the coming generations.

(l) *"his intellect and his emotions were clearly separated...and he had not yet arrived at the stage wherein they become united again"*: Separation of intellect and emotion shows lack of coordination. This is a sign of immaturity. A person is fully mature when he is able to coordinate between his intellect and emotions. Imbalance in both intellect and emotions can create chaos in one's character. When a person is too emotional, there is no room for intellect or reason. So too, when the person is too rational, he discards emotions. Human beings go by both. To be fully human being, we need to be reasonable and emotional. Emotion strengthens our relationships and intellect tells us to what extend our relationships should go. If intellect fails then we will not be different from animals and if emotion fails, we will be like robots or automatons.

Summary of the Character of Farmer Oak

Farmer Oak also known as Gabriel Oak is a man who is able to understand and analyze situations. He easily acts without much seriousness, thoughtfulness and without tension. He is a man of average fashion who wants to appear before others decently but not too smart. His character is presented as "good". This means that he was neither a bad character nor very illustrious. He was 'just good' and good is the base for better and best. So, there is a huge room for improvement. He has not become better and still far from best. He is in a way just above bad. He belongs to a common character of the general people. As a Christian, he is not fervent and religious but goes to Church as part of his duty and not out of true love for God. He just passively attends the Church service. Though he is passive in the church, he is still better than those who don't go to church at all. At least we appreciate him for fulfilling his duty. He is a little better than the drunken section of the society and lower than the communion people (who lived a good Christian life) of the parish. The dichotomy in his character is clearly seen when his physical body is present in the Church but his mind is absent by thinking about what he will eat for dinner while sermon is going on. He is man trapped in "*Laodicean neutrality*" which means indifferent or lukewarm in matters of religion. He was neither cold nor hot in his religiosity. He practices his religious obligations but not too seriously. He is also a man of tomorrow and not today. He is a person who does not want to struggle at the moment but afterwards. But we do not know that afterwards is a reality for him because he is a man who postpones. Oak's character runs like a palindrome i.e., which can be read backward or forward. People can read him from any side, that is when his friends were not happy with him, he was considered as a bad person and when they are pleased with him, he is considered a good person. He is an exploited character. His character and reputation depends on others. Oak is a person known by his neighbours thoroughly. His neighbours were able to interpret him. This shows that Oak is very gullible and susceptible to manipulation. Oak has a sense of traditionalism. He keeps and preserves the things he has inherited from his grand-father and great grandfathers. Oak did not merely inherit the old watch from his great-grandfathers but also their generosity and love. There are so many good things (values) we inherit from our grandparents, great-grandparents and parents, we should preserve them like Oak and hand them over to the coming generations. Oak is a man whose intellect and emotion work independently. He is not able to coordinate between his intellect and emotion. Imbalance in both intellect and emotions can create chaos in one's character. When a person is too emotional, there is no room for intellect or reason. So too, when the person is too rational, he discards emotions. Human beings go by both.

100

The Detached Statesman

"Detachment is not that you should own nothing. But that nothing should own you." **– Ali ibinabi Talib**

William Ewart Gladstone was a British statesman and Liberal politician. He was one of the most distinguished statesmen of the 19th century. He was Prime Minister of United Kingdom for a record of four times. He also served as Chancellor of the Exchequer four times. He proposed home rule for Ireland and introduced in the House of Commons as the *Irish Home Rule Bill* but was defeated. This splendidly handsome figure, whose life was one of high moral rectitude, was for much of his life very popular. He was known affectionately by his supporters as *"The People's William"*. He refused all titles and honours and died as he had lived, just Mr. Gladstone. He was never popular with Queen Victoria who, when Gladstone retired after sixty years of service to the state did not even bother to thank him. Gladstone was described as a Marmite person - either one admired him or disliked him and the Queen fell into the latter category. One of the mysterious aspects of Britain's constitutional structure is the relationship between the Sovereign and his/her Prime Minister. There are weekly audience between the monarch and the prime minister and this is where they meet and discuss issues of concern and there can be agreements and disagreements. Queen Victoria and Prime

Minister Gladstone were both strong-willed and therefore, must have a lot of disagreements on these occasions.

- *In spite of the good you do, people will intentionally forget you. Do good anyway!*

101

The Divine-Centric Attitude

The other word for divine-centrism is *Theo centrism*. A person who is thegocentric in his attitude sees "*Theos*" (God) as the centre of all things. He sees that without God everything is futile and meaningless. As the Bible says in Acts 17:28, "*For in him, we live and move and have our being*". So, the central focus of our existence is God. Everything is possible because God exists. Religion came into existence because God exists and revealed himself through the creation. Today, we are able to see the beautiful creation because God has created it.

A theocentric person sees everything through the prism of the Divine. He sees human beings as not merely human beings but as *Theophorous* (beings that possess or bear the Divine). Human beings are of immeasurable worth because there is a spark of the Divine in them. The Hindus have a beautiful practice of greeting one another. They fold their hands and bow their heads slightly and utter the word "NAMASTE". The word

'NAM' refers to NAME or the great or supreme name - THE BRAHMAN (GOD). Folding hands is a sign of respect to the GREAT NAME and bowing the head is a sign of worship to the GREAT NAME that lives in every human heart and uttering the word of NAMASTE is calling on the NAME of GOD. In other words, whenever I greet a person, I am recognizing, respecting, and worshipping the name of GOD who dwells in that person. Since, every human person carries God, I respect and love human beings. Isn't it beautiful to greet one another NAMASTE, every time that we meet each other!

- *Human beings are of great value because they are Theophorous beings!*

102

The Dodo

The Dodo (Raphuscucullatus) was a ratitae bird that lived on the island of Mauritius. Related to pigeons and doves, it stood about a meter tall (three feet), lived on fruit and nested on the ground. Ornithologists said that the dodo bird had all food available and enjoyed the climate of the island. As a result, the dodo had no need to migrate to other lands for food and climate. Gradually, it lost its ability to use its wings. Colonizers came to the island and brought with them hunting dogs. The colonizers with their dogs preyed on them and finally the bird came to be extinct. The extinction took place in the mid-to-late 17th century.

Today, this bird is used as the archetype of an extinct species because its extinction occurred during recorded human history and was directly attributable to human activity. The adjective phrase *"as dead as a dodo"* means undoubtedly and unquestionably dead. The verb phrase *"to go the way of the dodo"* means to become extinct or obsolete, to fall out of common usage or practice or to become a thing of the past.

This story of the dodo is a very poignant and moving story. If the dodo had used its wings constantly, it would have surely escaped death and extinction. It also would have lived to this day. Its story teaches us that every person is endowed with gifts and talents. These latent gifts and talents need to be explored and developed. If these gifts are not explored, developed and used, they will be *as dead as the dodo*. Let us therefore, not go *the way of the dodo*. Anything that is not used is as good as dead. Every person is endowed with talents, abilities, and skills. God has provided the raw materials in the form of desires and interests and the duty of each person is to discover and explore these desires and interests and develop them to the fullest. But if these abilities are not explored and developed, it will never find expression and it will be *as dead as the dodo.*

- *Any gift that is not used is dead and any ability that is not explored is lost forever.*

103

The Human-Centric Attitude

The other word for human-centrism is anthropocentrism. For a person who is anthropocentric in his attitude sees that the human person is the centre of all things. Everything in the world has meaning only in relation to human beings. In other words, without human beings all other beings and things are meaningless. The central focus of our existence is the human person. Everything is possible because human beings exist. Religion and Science are also the result of the fact that human beings exist. The curiosity of human beings has explored everything that they are capable of. If there were no human beings, there will be no one to reason the things contained in the universe. There will be no one to appreciate the beauty of creation. Today, we see the wonderful manifestations of the progress of science and technology because of the fact that human beings are. So, man is the measure of all things. Protagoras, the ancient Greek philosopher describes anthropocentrism thus: *"Man is the measure of all things" of things which are, that they are, and of things which are not, they are not.*"

If human beings are the centre of all things, we need to recognize the worth of each person. Human beings are surpassingly good and beautiful. Therefore, in any situation the value or the importance of the human person must be focused and elevated. Let us not equate a person's worth with just merely a few incidents and draw conclusion about them. Example, what a person says and does, presents only a fraction of what he is. Of course, what he says and what he does, speaks something of what he is! But to draw conclusion from just a few instances would be unjust because what he is, is so vast and unbounded that what he says and does is only a fraction of what he is. Let us not treat a person as valueless entity. Let us not devalue him by always pointing out his inadequacies. Therefore, let us be human when we deal with humans because only this will make us humane. A human person is the peak of creation and of immeasurable value. He is the measure of all things. Let us learn to respect a person.

- *Human being must evolve into being human.*

104

The Incident That Inspired Henri Dunant to Found The Red Cross

"Violence never brings permanent peace. It solves no social problem; it merely creates new and more complicated ones. Violence is impractical because it is a descending spiral ending in destruction for all. It is immoral because it seeks to humiliate the opponent rather than win his understanding; it seeks to annihilate rather than love. It destroys community and makes brotherhood impossible. It leaves society in monologue rather than in dialogue. Violence ends up defeating itself. It creates bitterness in the survivors and brutality in the destroyers." – **Martin Luther King, Jr.**

There is an incident that occurred in the life of one of the greatest philanthropists and pacifists of all time, who has left behind footprints on the sands of time. He is none other than Henri Dunant. The event that made him to take a complete U-turn took place on June 1859 when this young businessman followed Napoleon III to Italy with the intention of discussing water rights in Algeria. But in this unlikely circumstance, Dunant happened upon the scene of the *Battle of Solferino*. The battle took place on June 24, 1859 between France, Italy and Austria. Of three hundred thousand soldiers who fought for sixteen hours, more than one in eight were killed or wounded. Henri Dunant as a passer-by saw this and described it as "butchery".

"*Every mound, every height, every rocky crag,*" he wrote, "*is the scene of a fight to the death; bodies lie in heaps on the hills and in the valleys.*" The horrendous sight of the wounded and dead soldiers touched him so deeply that this incident became a turning point in his life. The massacre he witnessed there turn his business trip into a personal commitment to work for a permanent, neutral, international society of volunteers devoted to aid the sick and wounded during war time.

His book *"A Memory of Solferino"* recounting the affair and presenting his plan of action galvanized a society and within a year he and four members of a Geneva Committee engineered a successful conference in Geneva with delegates attending from 16 countries. Here the "RED CROSS" was born.

In 1901, he was awarded the Nobel Peace Prize jointly with Frederic Passy and he gave away his award money to charities in Norway and Switzerland. Today, the Red Cross that he founded has evolved into an international organization represented nearly by all the countries of the world and operating on a broad humanitarian basis through three organizations:

(a) *The International Conference* – This is its highest deliberative body which holds conference every four years.

(b) *The International Committee of the Red Cross* – It is composed of 12 citizens of Switzerland whose strict observance of neutrality enables them to cross international borders during war or peace.

(c) *The Red Cross League* – It facilitates cooperation between the worldwide network of 102 National Red Cross Societies. Their membership numbers over 170, 000, 000. The Bible says, "Blessed are the peacemakers..." (Mt. 5:6).

There is a difference between *peacemaker, peace preacher* and *peace wisher*. A peacemaker is one who actively involves and participates in a conflict situation with the sole aim of bringing peace and reconciliation. There is risk involved. He can be misunderstood and killed in the process of peace making.

On the other hand, preacher-preacher only preaches that there should be peace. He is engaged only in lip-service and never participate in the peace making process. While, peace-wisher only wishes that there should be peace. This is desiring or craving for peace only at the level of imagination. This is the most passive participation in the peace making process. Such person seldom takes part in peace making because of the risks and dangers involved.

- *Let us be peacemakers, not peace-preachers and peace-wishers.*

105

The Language of Love is Silence

"A fool is known by his speech and a wise man by silence."
– Pythagoras

Osho once said, *"The language of love is silence"*. When emotions run deep, words are no longer adequate to express it. Silence is the only way to understand and fathom its depth. When two lovers are really in deep harmony, in what Carl Jung calls as 'synchronicity', when their vibes are just synchronizing with each other, when they are both vibrating on the same wavelength, then there is silence. True lovers don't like to talk; they just want to feel the warmth of the presence of each other in silence. It is only husbands and wives who talk, lovers fall silent. In fact, the husband and wife can't maintain silence because language is the way to avoid the other. If you are not avoiding the other by not talking, then, the presence of the other becomes embarrassing. The husband and wife instantly release their ink like that of an octopus (When the octopus wants to hide, it releases black ink. Then nobody can see the octopus, it is simply lost in its own created cloud of black ink; it is its safety measure. Exactly the same is happening when you release a cloud of thoughts around you – you are lost into it. Then, you cannot relate and nobody can relate to you). Anything will do, but they release the ink around themselves; they are lost in the cloud, then there is no problem.

Osho also says, "*Language is not a way to relate more or less it is a way to avoid. When you are in deep love you may hold the hand of your beloved but you will be silent – utter silence, not a ripple. In that ripple-less lake of your consciousness, something is conveyed, the message is given. It is a word-less message. One has to learn the language of love, the language of each other's presence, the language of the heart, the language of the guts*".

Silence is the highest form of communication. If one learns how to communicate in silence, one will hear and understand subtle messages which comes from nature, higher world or the voice of the Higher Power. But the most difficult task would be to learn how to be silent but it is possible. Silence leads human beings to understand deeper realities of life.

- *Let us learn to be silent.*

106

The Laputans

In one of his peregrinations, Lemuel Gulliver, the protagonist in Jonathan Swift's *Gulliver's Travels*, visited the land of the Laputans. The Laputans were living in an aerial island floating in the sky. The floating island is about 4.5 miles in diameter with an adamantine base, which its inhabitants can maneuver in any direction using magnetic levitation. The inhabitants were highly intellectual people, who were preoccupied with the study of Science, Music and Mathematics which caused them to be so introspective that they had profound difficulty in communicating with one another. To cope with this situation, the Laputans appointed special officers called "flappers". The task of the flapper was to facilitate communication by taking a stick with a balloon on it and touching the mouth of the person who wished to speak and then touching the ear of the person who was to listen. "Those who are able to afford it keep a flapper in their family," wrote Swift.

Jonathan Swift was satirizing the intellectual elite of his time, who were obsessed with their intellective exercises. They have no touch with reality. The 'floating island' figuratively represents the mental state of those scientists, mathematicians, and musicians. They always live in the air not on the ground. They reside in the world of the imagination. They take delight in intellectual gyration, and scientific theories. They just locked themselves up in the world of ideas. They are not even aware of what is happening in the society and neighborhood. They do not even know what is happening below their noses. They live an insulated life - completely detached from the normal mundane life. Flappers are people appointed because they have become incapable of communicating with others on their own.

This is exactly, what is afflicting our world today. We have created an island for ourselves, where we feel cozy and comfortable. We have become highly individualistic. We want to do only our own things. The concept of the other is outmoded and troublesome. We prefer to live alone, enjoy alone, decide by ourselves alone and need no one. The advent of sophisticated electronic gadgets like smart phones has further alienated humans from each other. All prefer a *smart phone-centric* life. Smart phone has replaced friends, parents, brothers and sisters, and relatives. We have become self-obsessed *nomomaniacs* suffering from *nomophobia*. Now, what I need is that you 'leave me alone'. You do your business and I do mine. Do not interfere in my affairs and I too won't disturb you. Subjective rights and individual freedom have become supremely sacrosanct. The level of communication and interaction has gone down touching almost the zero mark. People don't feel the need for interaction. Each one is happy and busy with their own worlds. We are no longer in touch with the each other and the realities of life. Each one wants to live in their utopian paradise.

- *Why don't we try to communicate once again with one another and discover the joy of living together?*

107

The Making of Jeans

"I wish I had invented blue jeans. They have expression, modesty, sex appeal, and simplicity - all I hope for in my clothes."

– Yves Saint Laurent

No sartorial material has captivated the imagination of the modern youngsters as Jeans. However, the invention of Jeans is more of serendipity than design. It was the creation of an astute and sagacious business mind that didn't like wasting anything. His name is Levi Strauss, who was a young peddler. The story of Jeans began with the California 'gold rush' of 1849. The gold rush began on 24th January, 1848, when James Wilson Marshall, a carpenter found flakes of gold in the American River at the base of the Sierra Nevada Mountains near Coloma, California (present day Sacramento valley). With this, the news began to spread. Throughout 1949, people around United States borrowed money, mortgaged their property or spent their life savings to make the arduous journey to California in pursuit of the kind of wealth they had never dreamt of. All the people who wanted to hit the jackpot rushed there crossing vast distances of plain, forests, deserts and hills. As the American West was still wild to a great extent with no sophisticated modes of travel, most people went on foot or in bullock carts risking attacks from the native people whose land they were invading. People from other countries too began to flock to California. By the end of 1849, the non-native population of

California was estimated at 100,000 (as compared with 20,000 at the end of 1848).

Wherever people collected in large numbers there arose a demand for requirements and merchants and peddlers hastened there. Thus, Levi Strauss too, reached California loaded with goods. Among other things, he had brought was a huge stock of canvas thinking that people would need it to make it tents and the covers for bullock or horse drawn wagons. Strauss was being over smart. There was a little demand for his canvas and most of it was left unsold. Cogitating on how to get the load of canvas off his hands he observed that the pants, the prospectors and gold diggers wore got torn too fast. They needed something that stood hours of hard labour. He sought out a tailor and hired him to make pants from the huge stock of canvas he had. Well his business clicked. His pants were in high demand and soon he became a manufacturer of ready-to-wear pants which nothing could beat in durability. After a while he changed from canvas to denim and dyed it blue. People soon started calling the new pants *Jeans* as it resembled a dress material from an Italian city of Genoa.

In the beginning, Levi Strauss's business calculations didn't work out. His huge stock of canvas were no more in demand. But he didn't pack up his things and return. He continued remaining among the people and was thinking and observing how he could make use of his canvas and finally his creative mind hatched an idea and that clicked and his new creation was sold like hot cakes. What we can learn from this man is that at times, we concentrate so much on the closed door that we do not see the open window. Levi Strauss saw the door closed to his business but he was able to find out the window of opportunity open.

- *Have an alternative thinking always i.e., if one way fails, try the other.*

108

The Meta-People

"Brave people believe in a higher power than themselves."
– Lailah Gifty Akita

The *meta-people* are those people who are convinced that there is *beyond-ness* in everything. The original Greek word *'meta'* means *'beyond' (transcending).* So, we can call such people as '*people of beyond-ness*'. They are the people who are able to see the *noumenal* factuality of the *phenomenal* realities. In other words, they are the ones who are able to go beyond the world of appearance and see the true and deeper side of realities. In the phenomenal world (the world of appearance), we see concrete objects like the trees, birds, insects, flowers, humans, nature, the heavenly bodies or the galaxies and so on. But beyond all these appearances is the *noumenal world.* The meta-people possess the power to see the *noumenal* realities.

The meta-people are able to rise above the mundane banalities of life. They see every person as a *meta-reality or noumenal being* i.e., a person is not merely material but deeply beyond. A person is the epiphenomenon of the *Meta-Power.* They believe that everything originates from the *meta-world* and the real human strength comes from the *meta-world*. They depend on the *Meta-Power* that comes from the *meta-world* for their daily functioning of life. They link their mundane functions to the *meta-activity* of the *Meta-Power*. They believe that human beings who are in the phenomenal world can get strength and energy by constantly connecting themselves to the *Meta-Power* from the *meta-world.* One of the best examples is Jesus Christ, about whom the Bible says, *"In those days Jesus went out to a mountain side to pray, and spent the night praying to God"* (Lk. 6:12). Jesus was constantly connecting himself to the *meta-world.* He was constantly drawing his strength from the *Meta-Power (God).* He always linked his mundane functions to the *meta-activity* of the *Meta-Power*. Another scintillating personality of our times is Mahatma Gandhi. Can you imagine such a frail constitution could move and shook the foundation of the mighty British Empire? From where did he get such strength? His strength comes from prayer (meta-activity). He says, *"I claim to be a man of faith and prayer…"*, *"No act of my mine is done without prayer"*, *"But in all my trials – of a spiritual nature, as a lawyer, in conducting institutions, and in politics – I can say that God saved me. When every hope is gone, 'when helpers fail and comforts flee', I experience that help arrives somehow, from I know not where (meta-world)"*. Mahatma Gandhi was a man who constantly linked himself to the *meta-world or Meta-Power.*

- *Meta-people are those who transcend the phenomenal world.*

109

The Prank on Grandpa

Each afternoon Grandpa would lie down for a nap. One day, his grandkids decided to play pranks on him. They smeared a very small amount of chicken dung in his moustache. Quite soon he awoke sniffing an unpalatable smell and said to himself, "Why is this room stinking?" he exclaimed as he got up and went to the kitchen. Soon after he reached the kitchen he complained, "Kitchen too, smells." He then walked outdoors to breathe fresh air. Much to his surprise the open air brought no relief and he proclaimed, "The whole world is stinking!" When something unpleasant happens to us, we usually throw the blame on others. We never examine where the mistake lies. We start blaming those who are close by and finally blame the whole world for all the unfortunate happenings in our lives. That grandfather never checks on himself; he himself is not aware of his own mistakes. The bad odour is beginning from him but he went around looking for someone to blame. Finally, throw the blame on the world. If the grandfather had checked on himself, he would have discovered the chicken dung that got stuck in his moustache and then removed it. Instantly, the smell would have ceased. Blame throwers never find a solution. They grumble always and gradually become venomous and nobody can live around them. Craig Valentine says, "*Average people place blame, exceptional people take responsibility.*"

- *Most of the time we think the mistakes that originates from us began from others.*

110

The Principle of Giving

"I likes to give willingly; when I give willingly it enjoys me so much I give again." **An old German said in his broken English**

No human beings would survive without receiving gifts. All that I am and all that I have is nothing but a gift. My wonderful self, my parents, brothers, sisters, relatives and friends, Mother Earth, air, water, sunshine and so on are all gifts from God without which I cannot exist. In order to make me live He gives me oxygen by planting trees around me. Whenever I see a tree, I see how much God loves me. If God is not there, the tree would not be there and if the tree is not there I would not be there. God is so magnanimous. His gifts constantly and spontaneously flow. Some of the most valuable and essential requirements for human existence are all free gifts from God like air, water, and sunlight. God does not charge us for drinking water, inhaling oxygen and absorbing sunlight for maintaining optimal vitamin D level in our bodies.

God is the first Giver and He continuous to give. He does not stop and He cannot stop giving for He loves His creature and creation. If God stops giving, what would have happened to the universe? The consequence could be unimaginable. Suppose, God stops providing oxygen for an hour, what could happen to human beings and other beings? How do one know how much God takes care of each and every human being? Just by seeing one's plate of rice every morning, one can know how much God loves and cares for everyone. Have you ever reflected that every time you sit to eat your delicious meal, how did that plate of rice reach you? There is a great distance between the rice and your plate. That rice didn't come to your plate automatically or just by happenstance. For the rice to reach your plate, how many people are being made use by God, so that you can eat and live? This rice was sown in the field far away from you by the farmers who is not known to you. He ploughed the field, laboured hard in the rain and sunshine and not minding the dirty mud. There were many who helped him – people including animals. God sent rain and sunshine at the right time and made the seed grow and yield fruit. Then, it was ready for harvest and it was finally threshed. There are innumerable number of people who are involved in the process. Then, only it was taken to the granary. After this, the paddy was taken to the mill and after milling, it was sieved and finally it is transported to your town or your house and you are now able to get it. After you have bought it, you bring home and it's ready for cooking. In order to cook, somebody has to draw water, then, operate the gas stoves or collect firewood from the jungle. Finally, it is put into your plate. Now, do you see how many people are labouring and struggling hard every day just to feed you with a plate of rice and keep you alive? So, whenever you see your plate of rice always remember the sweat of the farmers and the love of God and you will never complain whether your food is delicious or not.

Today, we live because God gives us. God continues to give and shares His goodness with each of us through different people. God loves and cares for me through you and He loves and cares for you through me. So, without you, I cannot live and without me you cannot live. That is how God has made us so that we will help and share with one another. Let us be a gift to each other. Today, I thank you sincerely for what you have given to me. When you help me and when I help you, I feel a greater happiness. If God gives everything that He has to me, why am I not able to give a little of what I have to others? O God! Forgive me, let me not be selfish. You did not send me here on earth to fish but to share.

O God! Teach me to give because YOU alone know how to give. When YOU give, YOU give everything and YOU hold back nothing for YOURSELF. Why then whenever I give, I hold back something for myself. I really do not know how to give? Teach me YOUR WAY. Whenever I give at least I expect a "Thank You in return." Teach me YOUR WAY.

Here is a beautiful story of giving which I received some years back through an email. One day, a poor boy who was selling goods from door to door to pay his way through school, found he had only one thin dime left and he was hungry. He decided he would ask for a meal at the next house. However, he lost his nerve when a lovely young woman opened the door. Instead of a meal he asked for a drink of water. She thought he looked hungry so brought him a large glass of milk. He drank it slowly and then asked, "How much do I owe you?"

"You don't owe me anything" she replied.

"Mother has taught us never to accept payment for a kindness."

He said... "Then, thank you from my heart."

As Howard Kelly left that house, he not only felt stronger physically but his faith in God and man was stronger too which he had been ready to give up and quit.

Years later that young woman became critically ill. The local doctors were baffled. They finally sent her to the big city, where they called in specialists to study her rare disease. The renowned Dr. Howard Kelly was called in for the consultation.

When he heard the name of the town she came from, a strange light filled his eyes. Immediately he rose and went down the hall of the hospital to her room. Dressed in his doctor's gown he went in to see her. He recognized her at once. He went back to the consultation room determined to do his best to save her life. From that day he gave special attention to the case.

After a long struggle, the battle was won.

Dr. Kelly requested the business office to pass the final bill to him for approval.

He looked at it and then wrote something on the edge and the bill was sent to her room. She feared to open it, for she was sure it would take the rest of her life to pay for it all. Finally, she looked and something caught her attention on the side as she read these words....

"Paid in full with one glass of milk." (Signed) Dr. Howard Kelly.

Tears of joy flooded her eyes as her happy heart prayed: "Thank You, God that Your love has spread abroad through human hearts and hands."

111

The Return of a Criminal and the Regress of a Saint

"Know that transformation sometimes begins with a fall. So, never curse the fall. The ground is where humility lives. Take it. Learn it. Breathe it in and then come back stronger, humbler and more aware of your need for Him. Come back having seen your own nothingness and His greatness." **– Yasmin Mogahed**

What a happy moment it is to see the restoration of a criminal to sainthood. Jesus once said, *"I tell you, there will be more joy in heaven over one sinner who repents than over ninety-nine respectable people who do not need to repent"* (Lk. 15: 7). This is the return of a desperado. All will be happy to see the conversion of a wicked person. Every time that a person turns from evil to good, the world grows more beautiful for wickedness is reduced and beauty is added. Can you imagine a world when all wicked people work hard in order to turn themselves into saints? What a paradisal world it would be! The glory of the world will grow.

On the other extreme, what a luctuous thing it would be to see a saint that begins to take delight in evil. This is a possible inference that whom you know today as a saint can be a criminal tomorrow. Such incidents are not rare. Alexander Pope once said, *"The worst of madmen is a saint run mad"*. Can you imagine a human person who is heaven's masterpiece becomes a dismantled piece? Every time a saint runs mad, wickedness aggravates in the world. Every time that this happens, the world is losing its beauty and glory for the good is being subtracted. Gradually, the world will become a hard and strange place to live in. We shall become a foreigner in our own land.

- *Let us subtract evil and add beauty to our world.*

112

There is an Unquenchable Thirst Within a Man

"It is better to be a dissatisfied human being than a satisfied pig."

- J.S. Mill

One of the differences between human beings and animals is that though both have some common biological needs like hunger, thirst etc., animals are satisfied when these needs are fulfilled, while human beings are not so even when such needs are met. Once hunger is satiated, another need arises and when that too is quenched, another one comes and it goes on. Their desires, needs and wants are limitless and unquenchable. They long for new and fresh things. Let us identify some of the hungers and thirsts that human beings experience. They are as follows:

- Economic thirst
- Political thirst
- Psychological thirst
- Social thirst
- Spiritual thirst

The ultimate goal of all these thirsts is nothing but to find HAPPINESS.

- ***Economic Thirst:*** Economic thirst is a thirst for money and wealth. Certainly, it contributes to temporary happiness. People think that if they have lots of money and wealth, they will be happy. But this is an illusion for money and wealth can't generate perennial happiness. This is the experience of the wealthy people. Many billionaires knew this and therefore, they began using their money for charity and uplift of the poor. They do this through foundations. Helping others is one of the main sources of happiness. The seers and the saints of old knew very well that money and wealth does not guarantee happiness and therefore, they had always detached themselves from it and its influence.

- ***Political Thirst:*** Political thirst is a thirst for power, position and fame. Some people think that if they are in position, power and become famous they will be happy. But this also is an illusion because there is no politician who is always in power or position or fame till the end of their lives. In other words, this also is ephemeral glory. Therefore, it is not a reliable method of pursuing happiness.
- ***Social Thirst:*** Social thirst is a thirst for relationship with other members of the society. It is a craving for the company of others. This type of people think that if they establish a good relationship with others, they will be happy. This is true to some extent because if a person is in good relationship with others surely, he or she will indeed experience happiness. But this also is only temporary for relationship is possible through the physical presence and expression and the physical aspect of a human existence is only temporary. It cannot give permanent or lasting happiness.
- *Psychological thirst:* According to the founders of Self-determination Theory, human beings achieve their true potential when they fulfill the three fundamental psychological needs - competence, connection and autonomy. Competence is about gaining mastery of different tasks and learning different skills. When people

feel that they have the skills needed for success, they are more likely to take actions that will help them achieve their goals. Connection means experiencing a sense of belonging and attachment (relationship between people particularly long-term relationships including those between parent and child or romantic partners) to other people. Autonomy is the ability to control of one's own behaviour and goals. Here, I am in control of my choices. Choices are important because they determine my behaviours and goals in life. Now, to achieve this will certainly lead to a fulfilled life but to reach this stage will be very tough and difficult for the majority of human beings. Certainly, a humongous number of people will not reach this stage of competence, connection and autonomy.

- *Spiritual Thirst:* Apart from being psychological, human beings possess a deep spiritual dimension. Human beings need a Power that is higher than themselves to satisfy their needs. Many people have this experience of the Higher Power in their lives and this has impacted them. Some called this higher power as God. The founders of religions like Moses, Jesus Christ, Mohammad, Buddha, Mahavira, Confucius etc., teach the same qualities of God as love, compassion, forgiveness, service, truth etc. So, the highest form of spirituality is the practice of love, compassion, forgiveness, service, truth etc. In fact, the happiest people in the world are those who practice these values. Through the path of love, compassion, forgiveness, truth and service, the seers and the saints experience oneness with God and the universe. St. Augustine of Hippo (354 AD) said, "Our hearts are restless until they rest in you". Only in God all our longings will cease. This is perfect HAPPINESS. God is the source of happiness and only in him true and lasting happiness will be found.
- *Which thirst would you like to quench?*

113

The Spiritual Experience of Blaise Pascal

"The spiritual journey is individual, highly personal. It can't be regulated. It isn't true that everyone should follow one path. Listen to your own truth." – **Ram Das**

BLAISE PASCAL was a French mathematician, physicist, inventor, philosopher and theologian. A multifaceted personality, who belongs to a pantheon of great personalities the world has ever produced. He had numerous achievements in life. One such was the invention of a large carriage with many seats. With this invention, the first bus line carrying passengers from one part of Paris to another for a fixed fare was inaugurated. One of his motives was to gain money to give to the poor since he had already disposed all his worldly possessions.

Pascal always had a religious bent. After his father's death, his sister became a nun in 1651 at Port-Royal. From 1652 to 1654, he turned away from religious interests spending his time with libertine friends who were gamblers, womanizers and freethinkers. Pascal invited his sister (nun) and told her that he had a great contempt for the world and people and did not feel incline to God. However, on the night of November 23, 1654, Pascal had a profound religious experience, which led him to devote the rest of his life principally to religious activities. The experience so overwhelmed Pascal that he wrote a

"MEMORIAL" of it, which he thereafter carried, sewn into his clothes to remind him of the event. A servant discovered it only by chance after his death. It said:

> *"From about 10:30 at night until about 12:30, FIRE. God of Abraham, God of Isaac, God of Jacob, not of the philosophers and the learned. CERTITUDE, CERTITUDE, feeling joy, peace. God of Jesus Christ...Jesus Christ...Let me never be separated from HIM".* He concluded his prayer by quoting Psalm 119:16 *"I will not forget thy word. Amen."*

After this spiritual conversion, his belief and religious commitment revitalized and Pascal visited the older of two convents at Port-Royal for a two-week retreat in January 1655. Thenceforth, Pascal vehemently defended the existence of God. Philosophers can be of three types: Theistic, Atheistic and Agnostic. Theistic philosophers are those who believe in God and argue for the existence of God. While, the atheistic philosophers are those who do not believe in God and argue against the existence of God. Whereas, Agnostics are philosophers who hold the proposition that God's existence can neither be sufficiently proved nor disproved. They are indifferent and nonchalant to the first two propositions (theism and atheism). As a theistic philosopher, Blaise Pascal had to argue against the atheistic and the agnostic philosophers and his best argument is contained in his famous book *"Pensees"* which means 'Thoughts'. As a well-known Mathematician and scientist, he felt the need to do something different with those philosophers who were trying to disprove the existence of God and so he studied spiritualism. As he was good in Mathematical probability, he put the first Decision Theory for what to do if God exists or not. Then, he named it *"Pascal's Wager"*. It is popularly known as *Pascal's Wager Theory* and he recommended that believing in God is better than not believing in God. Pascal says that he purposely kept the last chapter of his book - "The Miracles" which contains the *'Pascal's Wager'*. According to *Pascal's Wager*, it says:

- If you believe in God and later (after death) you found that God exists, then, you gain Eternal Happiness.
- If you believe in God and later (after death) you found that God doesn't exist, then, you lose nothing.
- If you do not believe in God and later (after death) you found that God exists, then you lose everything.
- If you do not believe in God and later (after death) you found that God doesn't exist, then you lose nothing. Therefore, it is better to believe in God than not to believe.

Some of his famous quotes:

- *"We know the truth not only by reason but more by the heart".*
- *"Know then, proud man, what a paradox you are to yourself. Humble yourself, foolish nature, learn that man infinitely surpasses man and hear from your master your real state which you do not know".*
- *"The heart has its reasons which reason knows nothing of".*
- *"Nothing which is not God can ever bring me to fulfillment".*
- "His last words before death*: May God never abandon me".*

114

The Story of Anupam Kher

When I was a small boy, I used to admire Mr. Anupam Kher, one of the most versatile villains in Bollywood. His biographical narrative is typically a story of the boy next-door. He came to Bombay like thousands of young people do every day, with stars in his eyes hoping to hit the big time. He was 26 years old, bald and divorced. No one would have given the boy from Shimla (North India) a second look. He rented a ramshackle room in a slum, where eight others like him shared his dreams. Kher went from door to door begging for bread. The year was 1981. At this time Mahesh Bhatt, a famous but struggling director was trying to make good commercial films and decided to cast Kher in the role of a 70-year old man in *Saaransh*. The film made Bhatt into a legend. Kher became an instant draw. An actor everyone raved about... no wonder at 35, Anupam Kher is the one actor in whose shoes everyone wants to be. Rich, famous, successful, all and all, from a scratch.

If uncle Kher can achieve the height of success from a scratch, why can't we give a try? Our poor background should never deter us from chasing our dreams. Instead, it should create a confidence in us that "there are people worse than my background who climb the ladder of success."

Anupam Kher had an interview with the *Times of India* (November 14, 2010)

God: "I find God in simple things of life. God resides in everything that encompasses us. I find Him in the goodness of people. God is a faith for me and faith is the only thing in life that keeps us going. I believe in optimism and being positive. Optimism is godly for me."

Connecting to God: "I connect to God through focus, concentration, happiness and being good to other people. Prayers connect me to Him. I do not need a visa of meditation to get closer to God. It doesn't matter that I am stressed or happy. I can chat with Him any time I want."

***Karma* and *kismet*:** "I believe in *kismet*, but *karma* is more important for me. When I was young, my grandfather told me, 'Hard work is the only way to attain your goals'. And all through my life, I didn't try to prove him wrong. There is nothing in life that comes to you easily. I strongly believe and advocate the philosophy of Bhagavad Gita, *'Karmkaro, phalki chinta mat karo'* (Do your duty without thinking/worrying about results). For me karma is supreme."

True contentment: "Being kind to people, to be able to bring joy to others' lives signifies contentment to me. Being passionate towards what you do, enjoying it and being happy is important too. You can't make others happy, if you do not enjoy yourself. So live, laugh and enjoy!"

- *"Successful people do what unsuccessful people are not willing to do. Don't wish it were easier; wish you were better." - Jim Rohn*

115

The *Tao* of Happiness

"Happiness is a state of mind. It's just according to the way you look at things." **– Walt Disney**

In the summary autobiography of Lao Tzu, the Chinese sage speaks about *"forever tarrying in purposelessness"* that is, have no purpose, wait quietly and be ready to keep that attitude forever. That is the gate of wisdom and the *Tao* of happiness. The moment you set a purpose or a goal that is the beginning of anxiety. You become anxious, restless and worried about fulfilling that goal. When you are anxious, restless and worried, how can you experience happiness? You are in motion and when you are in motion, you're tensed and when you are tensed, how can you relax and when you don't relax, how can you enjoy? Anxiety is *'the gap between the now and the then' i.e., the distance between the present and the future.* The more purposeful we are, the more anxious we become.

Many a times, the goal or objective, instead of being stepping stones to success, have become stumbling block that causes frustration. By projecting myself onto future horizons, I have lost contact with the present. And loss of contact with the present reality is the greatest loss in life. Goal in life is important but if one starts thinking only about it, then, it becomes a source of anxiety. But keeping the goal and concentrating fully in the present by performing actions that will lead to the goal will generate joy. When you act this way, anxiety will disappear because you're fully concentrating on the present that will lead to a better future.

- *While looking ahead, we must be fully aware of each step that we take.*

116

The Unique *Me*

It is a good question to ask, "Who am I?" Am I only just a random collocation of some wandering atoms? Or Am I something that contains an element of uniqueness? All I want is to discover my unique way of expressing my 'self' in the universe. I have a passionate desire to be *Me*. It's a fact that my environment is exerting a strong *influence* over me – parents, teachers, elders, authorities, customs, traditions, books, media and so on. All these help me to be *Me* to some extent. But should I be limited only to their influence or transcend them? If I follow their diktats, I will be only a fine replica created by conventions and traditions. But that is not what I want to be. I want to be a free, different and unique person, belting out my own song which has never been sung in the whole universe. In case, if I am not able to create my own uniqueness, I will be only a mere replica of those personalities who have been manufactured by traditions and conventions. I would be only the result of conventional norms set by the society. In other words, I will be only a bounded and dictated 'self'. I know I cannot be *Me* without *influences* (tradition, convention and environment) but I should rise above these *influences* and discover the unique *Me*. The *influences* can help and support me for creating who I want to be to a certain extent. *Influences* are only a facilitator and not dictator. When *influences* act as a dictator, I cannot be what I want to be; I will only become the normal somebody who is expected by the society - a by-product of traditions and conventions. My personality is at the behest of the society and that is not the real *Me*. This is the reason why the majority of the people in the society are living a life of incarceration and imitation. Only a miniscule minority have transcended these *influences* and have discovered their uniqueness and are celebrating life.

> *"For centuries we have been spoon-fed by our teachers, by our authorities, by our books, our saints. We say, 'Tell me all about it – what lies beyond the hills and the mountains and the earth?' and we are satisfied with their descriptions which means that we live on words and our life is shallow and empty. We are second-hand people. We have lived on what we have been told, either guided by our inclinations, our tendencies or compelled to accept by circumstances and environment. We are the result of all kinds of influences and there is nothing new in us, nothing that we have discovered for ourselves, nothing original, pristine, clear...."*
>
> **– J. Krishnamurti**

117

Transformation Shop

"One new perception, one fresh thought, one act of surrender, one change of heart, one leap of faith, can change your life forever."

– Robert Holden

On the transformation shop was inscribed in bold letters, *"LOVE SOLD HERE, FREE OF COST."* A passer-by saw this and gave a guffaw and mocking remarks at the shopkeeper and shouted, "What a fool you are to sell love!" He passed a barrage of invectives. The serene and calm shopkeeper at once made a very delectable cool drink and gave to his impatient passer-by in the meantime. The passer-by took the drink and after having satiated his thirst said, "What an invigorating drink!" Then, as he was about to pay the money for the drink, the shopkeeper said, "I don't charge money for I sell love free of cost. Love does not tax people. I am here to help the weary travellers." As the passer-by went on his way, he said to himself, "What a fool am I? I laughed at the shopkeeper. It was actually I, who was to be laughed at!" Since this shop has transformed many people's lives, it came to be known as *"Transformation Shop"*.

This story tells us not to be rash and impetuous with regards to our words and actions. It teaches us to be more circumspective, careful, beware and alert. If we live our lives perfunctorily, it will end up in randomness and stochasticity. Mistakes are committed as a result of being random and rash with our own words and actions. The best thing to do is follow the old proverb that says, "Look before you leap". It would be foolish to leap in the dark and harm ourselves. It is always better to evaluate our words and actions before we cause negative surprises to others. We should never jump into things without any forethought. Some people have the tendency to act swiftly without much thinking and finally, hurt themselves and others. Therefore, what is important is "LOOK!". 'LOOK' metaphorically means to see and think carefully. If we always see and think carefully before we speak and act, we can avoid blunders, lapses, miscalculations and errors. This will help us to avoid making gigantic mistakes in life which can cause fatally humongous consequences on ourselves and others. Grave mistakes have lasting consequences on oneself, one's family and others.

- *Measuring one's words and actions will always keep oneself far away from committing fatal mistakes.*

118

Two Ways of Looking at a Person: Subject or Object

"If you change the way you look at things, the things you look at change."
– **Wayne Dyer**

A human person can be looked at from two perspectives: as a SUBJECT or an OBJECT! Philosophically, a *subject* is a being who has a unique consciousness or personal experiences or an entity that has a relationship with another entity. In short, subject refers to a human person. While an *object* is not a person but a 'thing' which can be possessed or manipulated by the subject (owner). An object here refers to a commodity, an item or a property owned by the subject. In real life, to look at somebody as an object means to fail to treat a human being as a person. Here, a person is seen only as an object and not subject. There are many rich and powerful people who use and manipulate the poor and marginalized in this way. The poor and the downtrodden are treated as mere objects. On the other hand, there are some people who look at other people as *subjects* and see them as persons like themselves. To treat a person as a subject is to treat others as we treat ourselves. This is the respect due to every human person. When we do this, we are only giving what is due to the person and not something extra. A human person is as worth and important as we consider ourselves to be. We must treat every person as a SUBJECT and not as an OBJECT. We must build, practice and operate on ***subject-to-subject relationship*** in our dealings with all human persons. This Subject-to-Subject approach is beautifully expounded by Martin Buber, the famous existentialist philosopher as the "I – THOU" relationship (Subject to subject relationship) and the obverse he describes as "I – IT" relationship (Subject to object relationship).

In the "I – THOU" approach, I relate with the other person as a *subject*. I respect him as I respect myself. In the "I – IT" approach, I relate with the other person as an *object*. Here, I consider the other person as only a commodity or an item or a property. Here, the person is not he/she but 'IT' (object). The best example of "I - IT" relationship is that of a master and his slave. The slave is the personal property of the master. The master has the right to keep and dispose of as he wants. In the 18th century Virginian Slave Market, the slave-masters used sly sales technique by making the slaves put on new aprons. To push prices higher, the owners always made sure slaves looked their best before selling them. Thin ones would be specially fattened up. The most horrendous effect of this slave system was that members of the same family would be bought off by different auction bidders. As a result, husband and wife, parents and children, brothers and sisters had to part with each other never to meet again. Their family-hood was robbed off. Here, the blacks were treated as mere objects. They are only commodities or market items. In this slave system, the blacks were considered as objects owned by their subjects - the Whites. Every human person is a subject and not an object. He deserves to be treated as a subject. The way we relate with others will reveal who we are. Let us learn from poets and all lovers of nature who treat all objects of the universe as subjects. The term they used is *personification* which means to treat animate and inanimate objects as having human feelings with whom one can relate. Objects are seen as human persons. William Wordsworth could see the Daffodils "*fluttering and dancing in the breeze"*. St. Francis of Assisi called some of the celestial bodies as *Sister Moon, Brother Sun* etc. Today, some pet dogs are christened a more lovely and affectionate names than human beings and loved more than human persons. I think human beings deserve a better treatment than the way they are treated now.

- *Who you are can be known from the way you treat others!*

119

Understand Your Body

"Respect your body, even with your thoughts. Be grateful for the body you're in. Be kind to it, nourish it, and nurture it. You don't get another one."
– Unknown

In his book *"The Discipline of Transcendence"* Osho speaks about the need to understand our biological clock. According to him, our body needs at least two hours of sleep during which the human body temperature falls below two degrees every night. And resting at these hours is the best time for rejuvenation and well-being of the body.

Let us see, what does Osho has to say in this matter: "I have come to understand my body. I have come to feel its needs. I have learned much by listening to it. I have tried all sorts of things in my life. I have been continuously experimenting just to feel where my body fits perfectly. Once I used to get up early at 3 o' clock in the morning. Then at four o' clock, then at five o' clock. Now I have been getting up at six for many years. By and by I watched what fits with my body. One has to be very sensitive. Now physiologists say that everyone's body, while sleeping, loses its normal temperature for two hours; the temperature falls by two degrees. It may happen to you between three and five or two and four or four and six but everybody's body falls two degrees in temperature every night. Those two hours are the deepest for sleep. If you get up in between those two hours, you will feel disoriented the whole day. You might have slept six, seven hours; that makes no difference. If you get up between those two hours when the temperature was low, then you will feel sleepy, yawning, the whole day tired. You will feel that something is missing. You will be more disturbed. The body will feel unhealthy. If you get up exactly after two hours, when those two hours have passed that is the right moment for you to get up. Then you are perfectly fresh. If you can sleep only two hours, even that will do. Six, seven, eight hours are not needed. *If you sleep only for those two hours when the temperature is two degrees lower, you will feel perfectly happy, and at ease.* The whole day you will feel a grace, silence, health, wholeness, and wealth-being. Everybody has to watch when those two hours are.

Don't follow any discipline from the outside. That discipline may have been good for the person who created it, but you have to find your own body, its way, what suits. That's right for you and once you have found it, you can easily allow it. It will not be enforced because it will be in tune with the body, so there is nothing you are imposing; there is no struggle, no effort. That's why I give you only one discipline and that is of self-awareness that is of freedom. You listen to your own body. The body has a great wisdom in it. If you listen to it and you go on enforcing things on it, you will never be happy; you will be unhappy, ill, ill at ease and always disturbed and distracted, disoriented. If it doesn't suit, then there is trouble".

Osho has spoken about getting familiar with our biological clock. Our body needs to follow a certain system or routine in order to enjoy health and well-being. Sleeping at the right and accurate time is one of the most important items in the biological clock in order to keep the body hale and healthy. Everyone must find out this particular time during which the body temperature falls below two degrees and make sure that their body rests at least two hours during that time. This is the best to rejuvenate and invigorate one's body. Loving our body is loving ourselves. It is because of the body that we are alive. We need to treat our bodies with respect. Once our body starts suffering, we begin to suffer and once our body dies, we die too. We love and respect our body by avoiding all that is harmful to the body - drug, alcohol, tobacco etc. If we love our body, we will be careful about what we eat and drink because what we eat and drink directly affects our body. We should not abuse our body if we want to live happy and long life. Our body is sacred and let us not profane it. It is the foundation of our existence and once the foundation is not strong, the whole structure collapses.

- *If you don't love your body; your body will leave you early.*

120

Understand Rather Than Laugh At!

Scientists say that forty-three muscles are used to frown. Should we use these forty-three muscles to frown at others?

Laughter is one of the most distinctive gifts that is bestowed upon human beings. This gift makes a human beings unique and complete. We don't see animals laughing. Laughter is a mark that distinguishes human beings from other beings. It is quite impossible to imagine a human person without this quality. It indicates, expresses and enhances our joy and happiness. Laughter has the power to cure our worries and anxieties. On the contrary, most often we abuse this great gift by laughing at the actions and mistakes of others. Often, we use it as an instrument for ridiculing, jeering and belittling others. I don't think laughter was created for this. We take delight in taking the Mickey out of others. We do this, at times, to put the other person down so that we can rise above them or at least the other person doesn't look better. This is a pharisaical pursuit. Sometimes, envy and jealousy can eat up our vitality.

Laughing at the mistakes and actions of others retards their growth and it also indicates the superficiality and triviality of our lives. Each time you laugh at the mistakes of others, know that you are impeding the process of their unfolding. A person who laughs at others must realize that he or she himself or herself has not grown to maturity. Those who block the growth of others are the ones who have not grown themselves. We need to improve and progress to create a better version of ourselves. We must analyze our own mistakes and contemplate on our actions and find solution that can make us better. Never show surprise at the actions of others however odd they may be, for there is always a rationale behind the actions of a rational being. Our duty should be to understand them. Most often we don't usually laugh at the actions of an insane person for we know that such person is a lunatic. But we easily laugh at the actions of a sane person; maybe we do not really know or understand the depth of human existence. Therefore, a person who laughs at the mistakes or actions of a sane person is either he himself is a lunatic or an angel. Here is pertinent to quote the words of Baruch Spinoza in his book, "*Tractatus Politicus*": "*Sedulo curavi, humanas actiones non ridere, non lugere, neque detestari, sed intelligere.*" (I have striven not to laugh at human actions not to weep at them nor hate them but to understand them)

- *Try to understand rather than laugh at!*

121

Update Your Knowledge and Attitude About Others

"Change is your friend not your foe, change is a brilliant opportunity to grow."
– Simon T. Bailey

The Greek fluxist philosopher Heraclitus famously said, *"Den boreite na beite sto idio potami dyo fores giati alla nera synechizoun na reoun"* (You cannot step into the same river twice; for other waters are ever flowing on). Every time you step into the river, it is no more the same water and so one cannot step into the same river twice. This adage explains the impermanence of things in the world. Everything we see is changing. Plato says, *"Panta chorei kai ouden menei."* (Everything changes and nothing remains still). Change is a reality that operates not only in nature but in human beings too. Human beings are also subjected to this reality of change. Therefore, we cannot but change. If flux is part and parcel of human existence, then I can't draw a conclusion that, what you have become today is not what you were yesterday and what you are today may not be what you will be tomorrow. You are unpredictable and contingent for change is constantly operating in you. And so am I! If this is the reality, then there is an urgent need for *mutual updating*. Unless you don't update your knowledge and perception about me and I don't update my knowledge and perception about you, you and I will become obsolete and we will never know the truth about each other. In other words, we will become outmoded. So, to have a profound understanding of each other, we need to take a little pain to update one another. This will deepen our knowledge of each other and our relationship. At the same time, let us not make anticipatory assumption about each other i.e., since one is like this today, we don't conclude he/she will be the same tomorrow. Let us not take each other for granted? Let us not determine or fix a person for he/she may change at any moment? If we are interested in each other, we need to continue updating one another.

If a tea prepared by the same person in the same way is different on two occasions, how much more so the person who makes it? In fact, it is the change in the person that is reflected in the change in the tea and that makes every morning different and every encounter unique. There is such richness in the human person that every facet is new and every spark a surprise. So, are we prepared to change and update our knowledge about others? If we are prepared then, every encounter with every person will be a unique, joyful and an adventurous experience. Carlos G. Valles has beautifully paraphrased this fact: "Perhaps the greatest sin one person can commit against another is to take him for granted. That robs him of his personality, his newness, his life. That is a psychological murder; it is not allowing my brother to be himself and therefore not allowing him to be. I have frozen him in the files of my past and have put him into my comfortable memory, easy to deal with along in predictable patterns. Very convenient for business and very unfair for life. My brother is alive and he fits into no pattern and must be allowed to show me today the face he wants to show. It is a crime to make him a mummy." Bernard Shaw once said, *"My tailor is the wisest of all persons who come to see me. Every time he comes, he takes new measurements."* Measure the man anew. Look at your brother with a fresh eye. Do not classify him; do not label him as though he was a biological specimen. So, do not dismiss him in your mind telling yourself:

"I know what he is thinking, I know what he is going to say, and I know how he reacts; I can spare myself the trouble of asking him, because he has always been the way I know him and will always be. Not in vain have we been so many years together. Give him a chance.

And above all, give yourself the chance of looking at persons and things anew. This new and fresh way of looking at persons and things is what is known as *UPDATING.* You are the loser when you don't update or take people for granted. You miss the newness of life in things and in persons all around you and condemn yourself to an outdated humdrum existence.

- *Update and be up-to-date!*

122

Violence

"Man's inhumanity to man
Makes countless thousands mourn!"

- Robert Burns

David Hume, a British thinker said, *"Look round this universe... inspect more narrowly these living creatures...how hostile and destructive to each other...how contemptible or odious to the spectator...."* There is no being more hostile and destructive to each other than human beings. Human history is fraught with violence. Violence is generated by man and he himself is the victim. *"Non-violence is the law of our species and violence is the law of the brute"* said Gandhi. Violence always generates disaster and catastrophe beyond measure. Violence has become a common feature in our world today. The strong takes pride in violence and the weak is in constant fear and anxiety. Here is a pitiable scene of a Tibetan peasant, a victim of violence who was secretly interviewed for British Television. He recounts thus:

> *"When the Chinese first came in 1950, they gave the farmers tools and they said they had come to help us. But four years later had taken control of everything themselves and pushed the Tibetans to the outskirts. My family is an example—two jumped in the water and committed suicide; one died in prison; one hanged himself. All my lands were taken away. These events should never happen to any human being".*

Here is another incident of a young nun beaten up by Chinese police following the riots of March 1988, interviewed for British Television in 1988:

> *"I was taken handcuffed to the police station. I was thrown on the floor and they stamped on my face repeatedly, beat me with an electric prod and kicked me in my chest. We were then stripped naked and three or four people continued to poke us with electric prods. We were told that as we opposed the Chinese we would be executed".*

Man's inhumanity to man has caused countless thousands mourn. This is what violence does. The great world wars took place as a result of man's hostility towards each other. Violence is as old as human beings themselves and it is caused by man and it will continue if humans do not stop. Everyone knows that violence is destructive yet violence continues to operate throughout human history. It is the mind of man that engenders violence. Therefore, if violence starts from the mind, it has to be stopped in the mind first. This is every individual's duty. Each one must stop the violence within himself. Mikhail Gorbachev, one of the greatest Soviet leaders who ended Cold War and open the road to freedom for Eastern Europe said, "*We are all passengers aboard one ship, the Earth, and we must not allow it to be wrecked. There will be no second Noah's ark*".

123

What is Needed is Understanding not Knowledge

"Understanding is deeper than knowledge. There are many people who know you, but there are very few who understand you."

– Unknown

Let us analyze the statement: "*It is so sad to hear the sudden demise of your beloved Mother!*" Is this sentence a knowledge or understanding? Or When you are in such a situation which one (either knowledge or understanding) really touches you? What is the difference between knowledge and understanding? When we talk of knowledge it refers to something related to the mind. It can be a piece of information that a person receives from a teacher, book or media etc. Example, (a + b)2 = a2 + 2ab + b2. This is an example of Mathematical knowledge but has nothing to do with emotion or feeling. This is pure reason. While, understanding refers to something related to the heart. The heart does not reason out as the mind does, but it only *feels.* We can touch the feelings of people only through the warmth of our hearts. Without feelings, relationship would be too dry, hard and devoid of sweetness. Relationship becomes pleasant and invigorating when emotions of love, compassion, sympathy, and empathy are attached to it. Let us analyze these common complains of people:

(a) "He knows me but he does not care."

(b) "He does not know me but he cares a lot."

(c) "He knows my problem but he does not care to help me."

(a) Analysis of the first sentence:

'He knows me': This means that the person has sufficient information about me (knowledge).

'*but does not care*': This refers to lack of understanding. This means, in spite of having sufficient information about me, he doesn't bother. He doesn't understand me. He doesn't have a feeling of concern for me. In other words, he has knowledge about me but no understanding.

(b) Analysis of the second sentence:

'He does not know me': The person has no information about me. There is lack of knowledge.

'but he cares for me': There is understanding. Here the person is not known to me but seeing my problem or situation, he tries his best to help me out. This is understanding the other person.

(c) Analysis of the third sentence:

'He knows my problem': Here, the person has not only information about me but he has deeper awareness of my situation too. He knows not only me but my problem too.

'but does not care to help me': Here, again, there is no understanding. What we find in the third sentence is that knowledge does not lead to understanding. Knowledge need not necessarily lead to understanding. I may know you but never understand you.

Here, we see clearly the difference between knowledge and understanding. There is a huge chasm between them. Therefore, I must consciously put effort to bridge the gap between knowledge and understanding. Knowledge must lead to understanding. Knowledge must create a feeling and feeling must lead to action. Only when I feel, I act. Example, when I feel hungry, I eat. Understanding leads to action. So, knowing must lead me to feel and feeling must lead me to act. This is called 'being human'.

In a relationship, what people are craving for, is not knowledge but understanding. Without knowing you, I can understand you as it is given in the second sentence (b). It is better to understand a person without knowing than knowing a person without understanding. Most of the relationships do not sustain because of the absence of understanding. The most common complain between friends, married couples, parents and children, employers and employees, teachers and students is *"He or she does not understand me. My dad or mom does not understand me. My children don't understand me. My boss doesn't understand me. My husband or wife doesn't understand me."* This is the beginning of breakdown in relationships. If you want to sustain and enjoy relationship, you should be more understanding than anybody else. Now, how do you practice understanding? The first step is to read the word 'understanding' in the obverse. Then, UNDERSTANDING becomes STANDING-UNDER. Practice *standing-under* the other person and make it as a part of your relationship strategy; then, hurts can be easily mended. So, if one needs to sustain and strengthen relationship, a bit of humility is required. Humility is not a weak virtue. Only the brave practices. If you conduct a humility test randomly, many will fail but only those who have strong spiritual values (love, humility, forgiveness, truth, peace) will pass the test. Where there is no humility, ego rules. Wherever, ego rules, relationship breaks down and never lasts. Whenever and wherever there is an argument (ego clash), tell yourself, "It's alright to lose an argument". By winning an argument against your friend, wife or husband, or Boss, you are not going to get a national award. Why argue so vehemently. It's a profitless exercise. Knowingly, when you give victory to the other person, it won't hurt you because you're doing it on purpose. You can do this only if you are opulent in understanding. Humility is the greatest enemy of ego and ego will try its best to make a mockery of humility wherever it finds so that it does not prosper. In the final analysis, the solution to problems lies neither in action nor in inaction but in *understanding*, for where there is *understanding*, there is no problem.

- *Learn how to stand-under (opposite of under-stand) others.*

124

What is Your Attitude?

"If you don't like something, change it. If you can't change it, change your attitude."
– Maya Angelou

Once Pirandello, a distinguished satirist and humorist said that if you see a 60-year-old woman puffed up with a fancy dress and with a face painted an inch thick with cosmetics, you can probably have one of the following two attitudes towards her:

1. *You can laugh at her and at the same time condemn her for folly in trying to look like a young girl at the age of 60.*
2. *You can laugh at her and at the same time sympathize with her for her unconscious recognition that beauty has left her forever and that she has to resort to such ridiculous make-up.*

Now, if your attitude is the first, you are a satirist– if second, you are a humorist. The first attitude is *condemnative* and the second, *sympathetic*. A *condemnative attitude* is destructive while a *sympathetic attitude* is palliative and therapeutic. A satirist is an uncharitable person not willing to bear with the mistakes of others. His aim is to correct people by directly pointing out their mistakes and follies in a strong and caustic manner. So, he condemns their mistakes and errors without least compunction. He is a person with high rationality sans sympathetic emotion. He thinks that he can change others through rigorous and pungent vituperations. The *means* (condemnation) he employs is so bitter that the *goal* (to change a person) is rarely achieved.

On the contrary, a humorist is a soft and light-hearted person who on seeing the errors and mistakes of others is instantly filled with sympathy. He is an embodiment of compassionate feelings though rationality is not absent. He readily bears with the mistakes of others and is fully aware of the perennial verity: *humanum est errare* (to err is human). His aim is to correct people by participating in their feelings and liberate them. This process of participation and liberation is what I would call as the *process of Empathization*. He is dulciloquent (sweet sounding) in his words that people readily accept him. The *means* (empathization) he employs is so sweet that the *goal* (to change a person) is always achieved.

The biblical parallel of the above-mentioned two attitudes is seen in the story of the woman caught in adultery (Jn. 8:1-11). There were two groups of people in the scene: The Scribes and the Pharisees on the one side and Jesus on the other. The Scribes and the Pharisees condemned the woman and wanted to kill her by lapidation (the penalty of stoning to death). But Jesus was sympathetic towards her as he said, "Neither do I condemn you, go sin no more". Jesus participated in her feelings and that liberated her. Life is touched and transformed through sympathetic emotional bonding. The Pharisees and the Scribes were condemnative, while Jesus was a always sympathetic.

- *Are you a Satirist or a Humorist?*

125

What is Your Weltanschauung?

"'Biblical worldview'. The term means literally a 'view of the world', a biblically informed perspective on all of reality. A worldview is like a mental map that tells you how to navigate the world effectively. It is the imprint of God's objective truth on our inner life." **– Nancy Pearcey**

Once, a pantheon of intellectuals was on an odyssey. The band consists of an economist, a biological scientist, a philosopher and a theologian. They were engaged in an intense debate on diverse topics touching almost everything from heaven to earth. Each one wanted to display their intellectual agility and acumen. Finally, they came upon a beautiful mango tree beside the road heavy with its fruits. The economist at once looked at it and said, "Oh, what a fruit! What a profit! These fruits should not be eaten but must be taken to market and sold". The biological scientist at once said, "We should not harm this tree for it is our life. It gives us oxygen". The philosopher then said, "This tree must have a cause. We should forget about oxygen and taking the fruits to the market. We must find out where does it come from and why it is here and what is its purpose?" The theologian then said, "Oh, what a beautiful tree and what a nice fruit! The work of God is so wonderful and marvelous. Let us eat some, sell the rest and preserve the tree for God has planted everything for the good of human beings".

What is your world-view? Do you look at things from a limited angle? Is your perception merely wrapped in mundane realities? Is your perception surpassing the phenomenal world (the world of appearances)? Are you delving deep into the realities of life? Can you recognize the *Immanent Spirit* pervading all things in the universe? See the hand of the Creator in everything. *Think deeper and look beyond and you will see there is a first Cause!*

- *Our weltanschauung should lead us to the Creator.*

126

Where Do You Reside?

"YESTERDAY is history, TOMORROW is a mystery and TODAY is a gift, that is why it is called PRESENT."

– Eleanor Roosevelt

In classical philosophy, time is divided into three distinct regions– *the Past*, *the Present* and *the Future*. The past is generally seen as immutably fixed and the future is at least partly undefined and as time passes, the moment that was once the present becomes part of the past and part of the future in turn, becomes the new present. Every human person lives and moves in time. He functions and operates in time. Time regulates his life. Therefore, time is of great importance to every person for he builds his life in time. Now, if one builds one's life according to time, in which part of time does one reside or live – *Past, Present or Future*? The Past, the Present and the Future are the three residences in which a person's life resides. A person can choose to live in any of these three regions of time. Some people choose to live in the past, some others choose to live in the present and still others choose to live in the future and some section of the people choose to take temporary residence in all the three. The last group of people is not sure of the ideal place to live. They live an oscillating life with a scattered concentration. They are fickle and have no fixed residence. They are like a rolling stone that gathers no moss. They have some goals in life to achieve but afraid to undertake due to the pain that entails it. They want only pleasure and avoid pain. Some people choose to live in the past because the present is too painful and the future is too uncertain and don't want to travel uncharted territory. They are afraid of pain and uncertainty. These people take delight in brooding over the past – what they had done, their moments of happiness and so on. Day dreaming is their hobby. They would avoid painful events of the past and select only the lighter ones. These people are seen most of the time dreaming and gloomy. They get ephemeral satisfaction by taking refuge in the happy events of their past life. However, they sink into desperation as they are soon transported back to the reality of the present. Such people usually don't accomplish much in life. Another group of people chooses to live in the future. They choose this because they are afraid to meet the challenges of the present. Most often they don't go back to the past because they might have had a sad and gloomy past. They are afraid to live in the past because their past is filled with painful events. These people avoid the Present because it involves a lot of struggles and pains. Therefore, they skip the Present and live in the ideal and chimerical Future. They will talk big things about the future – what they will do - their plans and dreams. But this type of people rarely accomplishes because they don't want to struggle and even if they begin, they'll soon give up as they are allergic to discomfort at the present moment. They will postpone everything to the future. They are idealists without pragmatism. Their common answer to any question is "Let us see!" They are the people who live in the world of tomorrow and tomorrow never comes. They make all kinds of promises which they would seldom fulfill in the future.

There are a few who have chosen to live in the present. They are people who have a lot of psychological stamina. They know that the present involves a lot of struggles and pains but they are ready to meet them. They base their life on principles like: "Life is a challenge, I must face it," "Life is not a bed of roses," and "No pain, no gain." They are ready to face any challenge that comes on their way. They have learned from the past and they put in all their energy in the present so that they will have a better future. They are so busy with the present moment that they have no time to brood over the past which they have overcome. They have clarity of the future and see it as a destination to arrive at. But they invest all their energy in the present that will make their *future* a happy one. They are firm in every situation. They are governed by the slogan, "No retreat, no surrender." They are the ones who win the battle of life. Such people are the ones who ascend the summit of life.

- *In which region of time, do you reside?*

127

Who is a Saint?

"The only difference between the saint and the sinner is that every saint has a past and every sinner has a future." **– Oscar Wilde**

I would define a saint as *"a holy person who is oblivious of his holiness"*. A person who feels and knows that he is a saint is no saint at all for this is a pompous and clandestine exhibition of one's pride. It is an unalloyed vauntiness. A saint never came to such a vaunty self-realization. A "holier-than-thou" attitude is not the attitude of a saint. *The saints never knew themselves that they were saints*. A person who is holy and knows that he or she is holy is still not holy yet. The only knowledge the saints had about themselves was that they were the most *"miserable sinners of all"*. Knowledge of one's holiness is ignorance of one's pride.

A saint is one whom people know that he is a saint. But the one who calls or demonstrates himself as a saint is only a pompous braggart far from sainthood. He is the progeny of the Pharisees or an *avatar* of hypocrisy.

128

Why Do You Follow?

"Be careful when you blindly follow the masses. Sometimes the 'M' is silent." **– Unknown**

Rowland Hill, the famous preacher once began a sermon thus: "The other day I saw a drove of pigs following a man. This excited my curiosity so much that I was determined to follow. To my great amazement, I saw them follow him to the slaughterhouse, so I said to the man, "My friend, how did you induce those pigs to follow you here?" "I had a basket of beans", said the man. "I dropped a few as I came along and so they followed me for the beans."

In life too, there are people who play the subtle role of the man who tempts the pigs to follow him to the slaughterhouse. The beans are used as 'bait' or 'trap' leading to slaughterhouse. If the pigs had known that they were being led to the slaughterhouse, none of them would follow the man. As soon as they saw him at first sight, they would run for life. People who use bait are manipulative and highly dangerous. If you are not wary, you will be trapped. This is why in life, if you don't work hard to become independent, you will become dependent on somebody. When you are dependent, you easily fall for the bait (a little money, help, support etc). The consequence is that you ought to please the provider or at least, you cannot hurt him. If you get more from him, then he will have more say over you. Too much depending on somebody is another way of reducing your power, dignity and autonomy. The best way to avoid being manipulated or used by others is to be self-reliant. Self-reliance means you work hard consistently, gain skills and achieve what you want to be in life. When you are able to depend on yourself, others will have less opportunity to come in and manipulate you in life. The saddest part is, when you don't have the competency and skills, you will greatly need the help of others to do your work and those many people coming into your life are not all sincere and honest. At least one or two of them will try to take advantage of you. This is how unhappiness comes into your life and at times lead to frustration. Self-reliance is the result of consistent hard work which leads you to acquire competence and skills in life.

- *Work hard and be self-reliant or you will be a chronic dependent.*

129

Why Worry About What Others Think of You?

"Don't let the noise of others' opinions drown out your own inner voice."
– Steve Jobs

Why do we continuously worry about what others think or perceive about us? We are constantly anxious about what our superiors, elders, bosses, friends and the society in general think about us or what opinion do they hold about us? We worry about this because we often desire acceptance from them and we want to know the level of their assessment or whether we rank well in their opinions. Another reason why we worry so much is that we are often insecure about ourselves and need confirmation from other people. We want to live up to their expectation. We think that living up to their expectation and ranking well in their opinion polls, will make us happy. So, we look for their acceptance. So, in this way, we spend most of our time pondering about what others think about us. But in most cases the truth is that people have no time to think about others. In general, people think about/for themselves or the things that are important to them. It is a self-deception to think that others are *always* thinking about me/us. They may think about me/us for some moments but not ALWAYS. Some people are so paranoid about people thinking about them all the time that they become fidgety and greatly disturbed. If people are always thinking about me all the time, when will they do their work or business?

There is a great danger in living according to the expectations of others. It is the worst form of modern-day slavery. When you act according to the expectation of somebody, you are enslaving yourself. Why should I think and act according to the ideas, opinions or expectations of somebody else? *You* are *you* and *you* are not *he* or *she*. Why should *you* become *he* or *she*? Why should you be dictated by somebody else's opinion? Why do you allow the territory of your mind-space to be ruled by someone else? Why should you think and act according to the expectation of others? Is it not a complete disorientation or alteration of what you are? If you do this often, your identity will gradually evanesce. The real 'you' will disappear and somebody else will be operating you. When you go beyond the expectations of others and fulfill your self's expectations, then you have become 'yourself' - the true 'you'. And this is the destination each of us has to reach. Sadly, in the process of trying to become what they want to be, some people some people landed up becoming what others are! This is the result of influence and imitation.

Our society is full of images and 'role models' that broadcast what is "in" at the moment. The media follows the young, beautiful, rich and powerful. People consume these illusions in great numbers. Everyone wants to be associated with the different role models that are presented before us by the media (consumerist society). The consumerist society is trying to impress upon each one that what you are, is not enough. You have to be above what you are – so see the young, beautiful, the rich and the powerful. Therefore, forget what you are and try to become like them. What you are is inadequate and you cannot fulfill yourself unless you adopt some of the methods or principles that they propose. The consumerist society presents everything as the ideal which in reality is only a mere appearance. This is the strategy they use for trapping the young.

The consumerist society is trying to rob you from what you are. It is trying to remove your original self and trying to give you an artificial glamorous self. It is trying to graft an illusory self on to you. Beware! Try to become what you are and never try to become what you are not. Be original, never be a duplicate or a photocopy of somebody else. Today, it is very difficult to find the original. What we find is only mere duplicates, imitations and Xerox copies. People especially the young have lost their originality and they are just satisfied being duplicates and photocopies of some role models. This adversely affects their society, their culture and their value system. In their imitation, they are adopting the society, the culture and the value system of someone else which may not fit into their own system. This is also one of the reasons, many are experiencing social and cultural alienation gradually. The young people today are systematically copying the great role models. They are too much given to copying that they are full of what they are not. As a result, there is a tension between what they are and what they are not. They are not able to balance between the two. Frustration is sneaking in and slowly destroying them. But the happiest and strong people are those who have realized who they are and they are no longer influenced by the opinions and expectations of others. They find their own way. These are the people who set new trends in life. They worked hard and discovered their values, and purpose in life. They know who they are and what they do and as a result, they live a happy, buoyant and autonomous life.

Finding out who we are is not easy job because from childhood, we have been raised in the midst of different paradigms and social expectations. We are expected to behave in a certain standard and become just like other people (the successful and the famous). It is hard to realize what it is to be our self. Rene Descartes, one of the most famous western philosophers, did not accept anything *per se* he reconstructed his own perception of his existence from real metaphysical fact – he might have doubted everything else but he did not doubt his existence. Descartes only accepted things he could prove by his own methodology and thinking. Descartes arrived at truth only by questioning. To arrive at the truth about ourselves, we need to question ourselves and our environment. 'Why' is a good question to ask for almost everything we do? Often, we accept everything at face value. As a consequence, we are filled with other people's ideas, styles and ways of doing things; we cannot distinguish ourselves from others. Being able to know and live in a way that we really feel is the right way of living. When we get the right answers from within, there is no need to look for acceptance from outside. Accepting ourselves and being contented with our lives are the most important steps in our existence. Are we ready to take the first step?

- *Acceptance is the password to happiness and expectation is the password to frustration.*

130

Why Worry About the Future?

"When thinking about life, remember this: No amount of guilt can solve the past and no amount of anxiety can change the future."
– Anonymous

Many people are so anxious about tomorrow that they forget what is happening today. They never live in the present. They spend most of their time regurgitating over the future. So, they lose the happiness of the present always thinking about the future. The imagination often transports them to the future as anxiety impels them to take flight to the non-existent or the not-yet-present future. The worries and the cares of tomorrow constantly afflicts and vexes their present and as a result, they lose all the peace and benefits their present could bring. Memory and history are the basis of whatever comes after it, so also is the future. The worries of the future often rob us of the enjoyment of the present. The imagination of what is going to happen tomorrow prevents us from being fully ourselves today. The image of what I could be in a more or less distant future dims the reality of what I am now. To be fully myself I have to learn to be fully now. Just as the past (memory and history) is the foundation of whatever comes after it, so is the future and therefore the thought of it, is indispensable in directing our life along the lines we want them to follow. But the danger comes when the planning outgrows the living and the dream overshadows the present reality. The wisdom lies in revitalizing the present with the gentle vision of the future.

Carlos G. Valles says thus: "A comparison: a good driver driving a car. He keeps his eyes on the road in front of him, the traffic, the car ahead, the traffic lights, the side roads; he casts a look at the distance to take in the faraway scene and gives simultaneous attention to the rear mirror to be conscious of what comes in from behind. That is, he has an all-round awareness with his immediate concrete attention on the situation just in front, quick to respond to any emergency in his steady course. If he starts looking at the beautiful landscape in the distance, to turn his head sideways to enjoy the sight, to look bodily back while driving ..... he is inviting an accident. The present can be turned into a tragic experience if the past and the future are allowed to rule our life."

- *Most of us come from the land of "Look Behind" and traveling towards the 'land of the Future' by passing through the 'land of the Present'.*

131

Work

"Who you are tomorrow begins with what you do today."
- Tim Fargo

Work is a panacea for all ills. It has the capacity to cure all ills. It maintains a person's physiological and psychological health in the pink. Many psychosomatic sicknesses can be remedied through work therapy. Work transcends the physical level and affects the psychological state of a person. Work is antidote to worry. A person who is absorbed in his chosen avocation has no time to fret over the worries and anxieties of life and be consumed with the anxieties about the future. Do not work for the sake of working. But perform your work with a purpose (productive). Do not be busy but be productive. If you are working so hard but reaping no fruit it means you have wasted your precious time and energy. Every drop of your sweat must not drop in vain but produce something. When you work sincerely with a purpose, it will give you hope and this hope in turn engenders cheerfulness. Only a person who works hard has something substantial to hope for. There is a lot of thrill and joy in waiting for the fruit of one's labour. That's is why when the farmer works hard and afterwards finds his crop so hale and healthy, he would simply smile because of the happiness he experiences within. He knows that he has not laboured in vain. Now, he knows that he is going to reap a good harvest. Only the worker can hope and deserve to reap the fruit of his labour. And, this hope generates joy. St. Paul of the New Testament says, "...Anyone unwilling to work should not eat" (2Thes. 3:10). A person who lives and thrives on the labour of others is an obnoxious parasite. Parasites are one of the most abhorrent and odious organisms. In the same way no one likes a parasitic person and such person will be hated by everyone. A person who doesn't sow, will never reap.

Chuck Close, is an American painter, artist and photographer. He is well-known for making massive-scale photorealist portraits. He speaks about work thus: *"The advice I like to give young artists, or really anybody who'll listen to me, is not to wait around for inspiration. Inspiration is for amateurs; the rest of us just show up and get to work. If you wait around for the clouds to part and a bolt of lightning to strike you in the brain, you are not going to make an awful lot of work. All the best ideas come out of the process; they come out of the work itself; things occur to you. If you're sitting around trying to dream up a great art idea, you can sit there a long time before anything happens. But if you just get to work, something else will occur to you and something else that you reject will push you in another direction. Inspiration is absolutely necessary and somehow deceptive. You feel like you need this great idea before you can get down to work and I find that's almost never the case."* Some people wait for great inspiration or idea to begin their work. But Chuck Close says that this may not happen to many of us. In such case, we don't need to wait and waste our time for an inspiration - *just show up and get to work*. If one starts working, inspiration and ideas come eventually in the process of doing the work itself. In the process of doing the work, one gets new ideas and inspiration. Therefore, what is important is doing the work. Concentrating on the process of doing the work will eventually lead to perfection and professionalism. Julius Irving in his interview with Budd Mishkin (NY1, March 25, 2007) says, *"Being professional is doing the things you love to do, on the days you don't feel like doing them."* Work is all about commitment - doing consistently whether I feel like or don't feel like doing it. Donald

Trump, the former American president says, "*Get going. Move forward. Aim High. Plan a takeoff. Don't just sit on the runway and hope someone will come along and push the airplane. It simply won't happen. Change your attitude and gain some altitude. Believe me, you'll love it up here.*" What Trump says is that one must begin the work - 'get going' and 'takeoff'. Don't expect others to come and help you. Your work is your business and it's nobody else's. Change your perception and it will take you to a higher level which will give you a sense of achievement.

- *Work and hard work lift human beings higher and higher.*

132

Your *Eye* is You

"Eyes are very different sometimes. We want to see something but they show something else." – **Kumar Aakash**

The Bible says, "Your *eye* is a lamp of the body. If your *eye* is healthy, your whole body is full of light; but if it is not healthy, your body is full of darkness." (Lk. 11:34). The eye is one of the most important organs of the body. Here, Jesus makes a distinction between healthy eye and unhealthy eye. Healthy eye refers to the healthy use of the eye. If a person uses his eyes positively, it will create positive vibration within him and his surroundings. What we see affects us either positively or negatively. The eye is one of the chief sources of information (data). The information is absorbed by the mind and is turned into thoughts, ideas and opinions. These thoughts, ideas and opinions are transformed into feelings (vibrations) and these feelings affect our body and that of others whom we interact with. In short, what we see with our eyes, affect our thoughts and these thoughts affect our feelings and our feelings affect our actions. So, if your eyes are healthy (positive), they will see positive things whenever they look at people and situations, and create positive thoughts which will create positive vibrations and the body will begin to feel elated and good. This is called healthy eye i.e., your body is positively affected by what your eyes have seen. On the other hand, if your eyes are unhealthy, they will only see negative things in people and situations. It will create negative feelings (vibrations) within you and people around you, will be negatively affected. That is why when you get angry, hate, and criticize, people don't come around you. This is because you emit strong negative vibration which directly affects them. People are more afraid to come near a violent man because he exudes a stronger negative vibration than others which can cause them harm.

The way we use our eyes will be exhibited by the condition of our body i.e., if your eyes are healthy your body will be full of light. If you have a healthy and positive use of your eyes, it will reflect in your body and vice versa. So, what is important is the way we use our eyes or the way we look at people with our eyes. There are looks which make us feel great, unique and elated. They inspire confidence and peace. This is a healthy use of our eyes. The eye is the lamp of the body which means without the lamp one cannot see anything in darkness. The eye is the thing that gives light to the body. That means a healthy eye creates a healthy body.

There are also looks that "kill us". They lead us to discouragement, dispiritedness, frustration and desperation because they condemn us. This is an unhealthy use of the eye. From ancient times up to our day, there are people and cultures that still believe in the EVIL EYE. It is mythical, yet, it conveys a lot of meaning. The Evil Eye is thought of as a look given to inflict harm, suffering or some form of bad luck on those that it is cast upon. It is a look which clearly states that, one intends something bad to happen to the object of one's focus either out of jealousy or pure malice. The myth of the Evil Eye holds that the malicious look is powerful enough to bring about actual disaster for the unfortunate person that is the receiver of the glare. In ancient Greece and Rome, it was believed that the Evil Eye was the largest threat to anyone who had been praised too much, or received admiration beyond what they truly deserved. The praised person would become so swollen with pride that he or she would bring about his/her own doom via the evil eye which was believed to be able to cause physical and mental illness.

This belief in the evil eye seems to be quite reasonable because when a person is too proud of his achievement, all the people around him will begin to hate and look at with contempt. When all the people around him cast evil eyes on him, somehow the person loses the grace. Here, people looking at him with evil eyes means they are all sending their negative vibrations to him and when he is bombarded with tons of negative energy, I think he will somehow experience the negative effect. When his whole surrounding is cursing him, the person will become graceless and will lead to disaster.

- *The eye is a window to the outside world. All information enters mostly through the eyes. If you want your body to be full of light, you need to be cautious and positively use your eyes.*

133

Youth! Dynamism is Thy Name

> *"Youth is not a time of life; it is a state of mind; it is not a matter of rosy cheeks, red lips and supple knees; it is a matter of the will, quality of the imagination, a vigor of the emotions; it is the freshness of the deep springs of life."*
> **– Samuel Ullman**

There is in every youth an *"Unfathomable Power"* which can be better termed as *'Dynamism'*. In some, this power is seen brightly and in others dimly. In a genius, this power shines brightest. This power is supposed to glow in every juvenile person and if it is lacklustre, it can be ignited or illumined again. We know that a genius is not born but made, largely self-made. He is the epiphenomenon of self-construction, self-discipline, self-moulding and s el f- development. H e goes through an evolutionary process, through a technique by which the source of dynamism latent in him is discovered, tapped, awakened, poured out and utilized rightly, efficiently and to the best of advantage and purpose. This power is like electricity manifesting itself through a bulb. This power though delitescent (latent) cannot find expression in a two-year-old boy because the equipment is not fully developed. In an old man, this instrument is worn out and therefore, dynamism or power cannot be seen there. So, Youth is the *Powerhouse*. Youth means *Power*. Youth cannot be lackadaisical for its name is dynamism. In a youth this dynamism is manifested in full force. Its potential is gargantuan, tremendous and almost limitless. As this power is so puissant and potent, it needs to be channelized for constructive purposes. Otherwise, it can cause a chaotic existential catastrophe as we have seen in the case of Hitler, the pathological egotist and Napoleon, the megalomaniac. These people mis-channelized their power and it eventually became destructive for themselves and for others. The best way to channelize this power is to set a positive goal or target in life, worth dying for. Once this goal is set, all the powers within one's self must be congregated for the accomplishment of the goal. If there is no set goal, it is bound to lead to confusion and destruction in one's existential fabric. The upshot will be one of frustration, dissatisfaction and unrest within. The unrest within the youth is always manifested in the form of violence in the society. Therefore, be focused in your life and use the powerful resources that are within you to realize your goals and dreams. Try to soar high in life. Remember the words of Seneca: "*Vita sine proposito languid et vaga est*" (Life without pursuit is a vague and languid thing). Know that where there is no goal, energy dissipates. You must work hard on your goals and achieve them - hone your skills and competence and contribute to the society. You are the foundation on which the future of the society is built upon. Tom Mann was an English trade unionist. He was largely self-educated and successful organizer and popular speaker in the British labour movement. He speaks about the youth thus: "*The future of the world belongs to the youth of the world and it is from the youth and not from the old that the fire of life will warm and enlighten the world. It is your privilege to breathe the breath of life into the dry bones of many around you.*"